DATA MODELING

MADE SIMPLE

A Practical Guide for

Business and IT Professionals

second edition

Steve Hoberman

Published by:
Technics Publications, LLC
2 Lindsley Road
Basking Ridge, NJ 07920 USA

http://www.TechnicsPub.com

Cover design by Mark Brye
Edited by Carol Lehn
Cartoons by Abby Denson, www.abbycomix.com

ISBN, print ed.	9780977140060
ISBN, PDF	9781634620406
ISBN, Kindle	9781634620154
ISBN, ePub	9781634620161

First Printing 2005
Second Printing 2007
Third Printing 2008
Fourth Printing 2009, completely revised
Fifth Printing 2016

Printed in the United States of America
Library of Congress Control Number: 2008910373

Praise for Data Modeling Made Simple

Steve Hoberman has created an informative, fun, easy to follow, and practical book sharing data modeling concepts which are essential for any professional involved in information technology. He clearly answers key questions behind the what, why and how of data modeling and reinforces the explanations with appropriate examples, analogies and exercises.

Len Silverston

Best-Selling Author of The Data Model Resource Book, Volumes 1, 2 and 3

Data modeling is one of the under-exploited, and potentially very valuable, business capabilities that are often hidden away in an organization's Information Technology department. Data Modeling Made Simple highlights both the resulting damage to business value, and the opportunities to make things better. As an easy-to follow and comprehensive guide on the 'why' and 'how' of data modeling, it also reminds us that a successful strategy for exploiting IT depends at least as much on the information as on the technology.

Chris Potts

Corporate IT Strategist and Author of fruITion:
Creating the Ultimate Corporate Strategy for Information Technology

Data Modeling Made Simple is an excellent training guide for anyone entering the data modeling field. Steve Hoberman takes the fundamental concepts of data modeling and presents them in an easy to understand and entertaining manner that I'm sure you will find valuable.

David Marco

President, EWSolutions

What a great book—and a fun read too! Steve has captured the essence of data modeling and made it simple. For those who are not data modelers but need to work with them, this book is an excellent primer. For those who model data occasionally but not routinely, it is an invaluable quick reference. And for those of us who are experienced (and incorrigible) data modelers, Data Modeling Made Simple is a terrific reminder that we really can keep it simple!

David Wells

Business Intelligence Consultant and Teacher

I have purchased several of these books for use in my position as a Data Architect and Database Designer. It is the perfect tool to give to both technical and business people who are new to data modeling. Steve has a way of explaining the complexities and fundamentals of data modeling in a way that people from diverse experiences and backgrounds can understand. If you have a need to quickly educate a person on data modeling, this book fits that bill. It has always been well received by those with whom I shared it.

Tom Bilcze
Lead Database Designer, Westfield Group

Data Modeling Made Simple is a must read for all professionals new to data modeling, as well as those who want to 'speak the language' and understand the concepts. Steve writes as though he is right there with you, walking you through the terminology, explaining the symbols, and telling you what you should consider doing before, during and after you have modeled your data.

Robert S. Seiner
President KIK Consulting & Educational Services, LLC and Publisher,
The Data Administration Newsletter, tdan.com

As someone who does data architecture every day, I sometimes forget why. I just know that I start with subject areas and work my way down. I need definitions that are useful, but sometimes find it hard to explain to others what I mean by that. I have adopted Steve's words and examples when communicating to others what I do and why I do it that way; and the best part is that people are getting it.

James Lee
Data Architecture & Reporting Manager, WebMD Health Services

It's the beauty of the book that it covers a breadth of material but at the right level to keep it short and accessible. The book is very readable (I did it in a few sittings) and employs an effective and understandable business card scenario for examples and exercises all the way through the book. The exercises give some good application opportunities for the material and there are practical tips and illustrative anecdotes throughout.

Wayne Little
CEO, Creative Data Solutions, Inc.

Contents at a Glance

Contents

Acknowledgements

There are many stars in my life who have brightened (and continue to brighten) my path.

Some are stars in the data management industry: Michael Blaha, for his knowledge of UML; Wayne Eckerson, who makes words come alive; David Hay, for his data modeling patterns and passion (and for his comments on the first edition, of which many have made their way into this second edition); Bill Inmon for his contributions to data warehousing and his vision on upcoming trends such as unstructured data; Dave Marco, for bringing metadata mainstream (and for playing a mean game of tennis); Bob Seiner, for advancing the field of data governance and for publishing Tdan.com, one of the most valuable journals in our industry; Len Silverston, for his Data Model Resource Book series, which has helped many of us jumpstart data modeling projects and improve consistency within our organizations; Graeme Simsion, for challenging us on how we do data modeling, and for providing practical techniques on improving how we work with others; David Wells, for his diverse skill set ranging from business intelligence to data modeling to teaching to mentoring to PowerPoint skills to photography to beer.

Data stars have also advanced our field through user groups such as DAMA. Through volunteerism, individuals organize monthly and quarterly meetings, arrange speakers, write texts – all to advance our industry and keep us connected. Just to name a few of these data stars that I have worked with over the years: Kasi Anderson, Davida Berger, Tom Bilcze, Michael Brackett, Jimmy Chen, Susan Earley, Ben Ettlinger, Deborah Henderson, Jeff Lawyer, Carol Lehn, Wayne Little, Mark Mosley, Bill Nagel, Cathy Nolan, John Schley, Ivan Schotsmans, and Anne Marie Smith.

Several stars have also had a very positive impact on this book. Thanks Bill, Graeme and Michael for your chapter contributions. Thanks Jeani, for reviewing the first edition of this text. Thanks Carol, for the superb editing job, Mark for the dynamite cover, and Abby for the great cartoons.

Several stars are even outside the world of data. Thanks Dad, for your integrity, work ethic, and problem-solving ability ("It's always cause and effect, Steve-o"). Thanks Mom, for setting the example of a teacher who loves to share knowledge. Thanks Jenn, for keeping my life sweet. Thanks Sadie and Jamie, for keeping me in the moment and reminding me every day to keep things simple.

A data model is the brain of an application, a conceptual framework that represents the business as accurately as possible. It defines the players, actions, and rules that govern the ways in which business processes work, representing them in a standard syntax that both humans and applications can interpret. In essence, a data model turns business concepts into computer code so that applications and systems can process information on our behalf. Without data models, we wouldn't be able to automate many of the processes that drive our organizations.

Given the pivotal role played by data models, it should be no surprise that they often determine whether an application is effective. A poorly designed data model can wreak havoc on even the most elegantly designed application. Poor performance, inaccurate query results, inflexible rules, and inconsistent metadata are just some of the results of a poor data model. A poor data model can hamstring an application.

On the flip side, a good data model serves as a lingua franca between business and information-technology professionals. It provides a shared understanding of the business that aligns business and technical professionals at the outset of a project. Conceptual and logical data models capture the ways in which technical professionals think a business process works. Business professionals can examine those assumptions and offer corrections and refinements before code is created.

I can't think of anyone better suited to explaining how data models work in plain, simple English than Steve Hoberman. Many skilled data modelers revel in the arcane art they practice and may as well be orbiting Pluto as working with business professionals. Not so Steve, who has demonstrated a mastery of making data modeling fun and easy in the courses he teaches for The Data Warehousing Institute. Although an accomplished data modeler himself—as is evident in his other book, *The Data Modeler's Workbench*—Steve is even more skillful in connecting with his audience. His enthusiasm and energy to communicate data modeling techniques is beyond compare. Steve is one of our most beloved and effective faculty members.

Meeting an important need. I'm extremely glad that Steve has decided to write *Data Modeling Made Simple*, because the need for this kind of book is huge. Given the importance of data models to the success of applications, it is surprising that so many business people (and more than a few technical people) lack understanding about them. This book will go a long way toward raising awareness of the importance and role of data models to organizations among business and technical professionals.

Specifically, business professionals who are sponsoring an application or have been assigned to the project team will find this book a useful primer on the topic. Technical professionals who are new to application design and development will find the book a quick and easy way to learn the fundamentals of data modeling. And professors who want to help their students grasp data modeling concepts, terminology, and success criteria will want to add this book to their required reading list.

Wayne W. Eckerson

Director of Research and Services
The Data Warehousing Institute

If you are like me, you usually skip book introductions and jump straight into Chapter 1. By calling this section "Read me first!" instead of "Introduction", I am hoping you will actually read this *first*. It will help you get the most out of this book by becoming familiar with the learning objectives and getting a glimpse of each section and chapter.

This book has ten key objectives:

1. You will learn when a data model is needed, and which type of data model is most effective for each situation
2. You will be able to read a data model of any size and complexity with the same confidence as reading a book
3. You will be able to build a fully normalized relational data model as well as an easily navigable dimensional model
4. You will be able to apply techniques to turn a logical data model into an efficient physical design
5. You will be able to leverage several templates to make requirements gathering more efficient and accurate
6. You will be able to explain all ten categories of the Data Model Scorecard®
7. You will learn practical advice on improving your working relationships with others
8. You will appreciate the impact unstructured data has and will have on our data modeling deliverables
9. You will learn basic UML concepts
10. You will be able to put data modeling in context with XML, metadata, and agile development.

This book contains five sections. Section I introduces data modeling, along with its purpose and variations. Section II explains all of the components of a data model. Section III dives into the relational and dimensional conceptual, logical, and physical data models. Section IV focuses on improving data model quality through templates, the Data Model Scorecard, and better communication with businesspeople and the project team. Section V introduces essential topics beyond data modeling.

To connect the book's content with the book's ten key objectives, Section I accomplishes Objective 1 on the previous page. Section II accomplishes Objective 2, Section III accomplishes Objectives 3 and 4, Section IV accomplishes Objectives 5, 6, and 7, and Section V accomplishes Objectives 8, 9, and 10 on the previous page.

Section I contains the first three chapters. Chapter 1 introduces the data model and explains this powerful tool using two examples (ice cream and business cards) which are both carried throughout the text so that the reader can appreciate the process of building a data model from requirements through design. Chapter 2 explains the two core characteristics of a data model that make it so valuable: communication and precision. This chapter then explores those areas where the data model is most effective. Chapter 3 compares the data model to a camera, exploring four settings on the camera that equate perfectly to the data model. Understanding the impact these settings can have on a data model will increase your chances for a successful application. (Note: An application is a program or group of programs (software) designed to perform a specific function for end users. For example, a word processing application, an order processing application, a profitability reporting system, etc.)

Section II contains the next four chapters, in which each describes a different component of the data model: Chapter 4 on entities, Chapter 5 on attributes, Chapter 6 on relationships, and Chapter 7 on keys.

Section III contains the next three chapters, which discuss the different types of models: conceptual, logical, and physical. Chapter 8 goes into detail on the conceptual data model, discussing the three variations along with how to build this type of model. Chapter 9 focuses on the relational and dimensional logical data model. Chapter 10 focuses on the physical data model, going through the different techniques for building an effective design, such as denormalization and partitioning. Slowly Changing Dimensions (SCDs) are also discussed in this chapter.

Section IV contains the next three chapters, which aim to improve data model quality through templates, the Data Model Scorecard, and better communication with business people and the project team. Chapter 11 offers some useful templates for capturing and validating requirements. These templates will save time and improve the accuracy of the resulting data model. Chapter 12 focuses on the Data Model Scorecard, a proven technique for validating data model quality. Chapter 13 provides practical techniques to the analyst and data modeler for working with other team members.

Section V contains the next three chapters, which introduce essential topics beyond data modeling. Chapter 14 focuses on unstructured data, which is fast becoming part of our requirements. We therefore need to understand it better, along with taxonomies and ontologies. Chapter 15 provides an overview of the Unified Modeling Language (UML). We conclude with Chapter 16, where I will address the top five most frequently asked questions in my classes, including discussions on XML, metadata, and agile development.

This second edition has been completely rewritten. All of the sections from the first edition have been revised and expanded with new techniques and examples, including the chapter on the Data Model Scorecard. This book also includes more on the process of building data models. Key points have been added at the end of each chapter as a way to reinforce concepts. Even poetry has been added in the form of a haiku, which is a three-line poem containing five syllables in the first line, seven in the second, and five in the third. Each chapter begins with a haiku that succinctly summarizes the chapter.

New terms such as 'Wayfinding' have also been introduced. In addition, clear explanations are provided for several vague concepts in our field such as metadata. I have also added some thought-provoking exercises, with answers provided at the back of the book. Also at the back of the book is a handy glossary and comprehensive index.

A nice feature of this second edition is that it includes more than just *my* voice. I started outlining sections on topics such as unstructured data and UML and then quickly realized that there are experts in each of these areas who can do a better job than I. So, Graeme Simsion wrote Chapter 13 on working with others, Bill Inmon wrote Chapter 14 on unstructured data, and Michael Blaha wrote Chapter 15 on UML.

Data modeling is more than a job or a career - it is a mindset, an invaluable process, a healthy addiction, a way of life. Remember to Keep It Simple, and enjoy the ride!

Section I introduces data modeling and explains the purpose of a data model and its many variations. At the completion of this section, the reader will be able to justify the need for a data model and know which type of model is most effective for each situation. The reader will also be able to perform a very high-level assessment of a data model by identifying certain characteristics of the data model and then determining how well these characteristics and the specific purpose of the model are aligned.

Chapter 1 introduces the data model and explains this powerful tool using two examples, both of which are used throughout the text. I love desserts and sweets, so one example will model ice cream (yes, ice cream!). The other example is modeling business cards. Both ice cream and business cards will illustrate modeling techniques so that the reader can appreciate the process of building a data model from requirements through design.

Chapter 2 explains the two core characteristics of a data model that make it so valuable: communication and precision. You will learn where communication occurs and about the three situations that can weaken data model precision. This chapter then explores the areas within the business and application where the data model can be used.

Chapter 3 then compares the data model to a camera, exploring four settings on the camera that equate perfectly to the data model. Understanding the impact these settings can have on a data model will increase the chances for a successful application. This chapter also compares the photograph formats to the three levels at which the data model can be developed: conceptual, logical, and physical.

How do I get there?
Maps, blueprints, data models
Please show me the way

I gave the steering wheel a heavy tap with my hands as I realized that once again, I was completely lost. It was about an hour before dawn, I was driving in France, and an important business meeting awaited me. I spotted a gas station up ahead that appeared to be open. I parked, went inside, and showed the attendant the address of my destination.

I don't speak French and the attendant didn't speak English. The attendant did, however, recognize the name of the company I needed to visit. Wanting to help and unable to communicate verbally, the attendant took out a pen and paper. He drew lines for streets, circles for roundabouts along with numbers for exit paths, and rectangles for his gas station and my destination, MFoods. The picture he drew resembled that which appears in Figure 1.1.

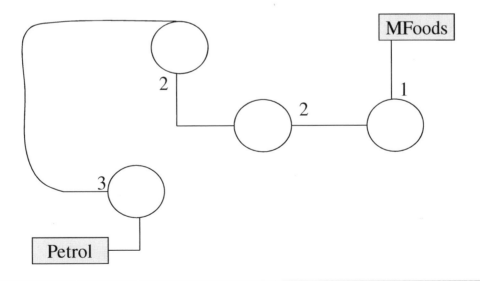

Figure 1.1 Simplification of geographic landscape

With this custom-made map, which contained only the information that was relevant to me, I arrived at my address without making a single wrong turn. This map was a model of the actual roads I needed to travel.

A map simplifies a complex *geographic* landscape in the same way that a data model simplifies a complex *information* landscape. This chapter explains the data model and its role as an invaluable wayfinding tool. It also introduces the ice cream and business card examples which are carried throughout the text.

WAYFINDING EXPLAINED

If the term 'data model' does not excite you or your business users, try the term 'wayfinding' instead. Wayfinding encompasses all of the techniques and tools used by people and animals to find their way from one site to another. If travelers navigate by the stars, for example, the stars are their wayfinding tools. Maps and compasses are also wayfinding tools.

All models are wayfinding tools. A model is a set of symbols and text used to make a complex concept easier to grasp. The world around us is full of obstacles that can overwhelm our senses and make it very challenging to focus only on the relevant information needed to make intelligent decisions. A map helps a visitor navigate a city. An organization chart helps an employee understand reporting relationships. A blueprint helps an architect communicate building plans. The map, organization chart, and blueprint are all types of models that represent a filtered, simplified view of something complex, with the goal of improving a wayfinding experience by helping people understand part of the real world.

It would probably have taken me hours of trial and error to reach my destination in France, whereas that simple map the gas station attendant drew provided me with an almost instantaneous broad understanding of how to reach my destination. A model makes use of standard symbols that allow one to grasp the content quickly. In the map he drew for me, the attendant used lines to symbolize streets and circles to symbolize roundabouts. His skillful use of those symbols helped me visualize the streets and roundabouts.

DATA MODEL EXPLAINED

When I was in college, the term 'information overload' was used to mean our brains had reached the maximum amount of words spoken by the professor, appearing on her flipcharts, and in the page of notes in front of me. It was time for a stroll around campus, a game of tennis, or a couple of quarters in Space Invaders to get my mind recharged and ready for more. Today however, it seems we are creating and receiving more and more information, and taking fewer and fewer breaks. I have heard it quoted several times that the amount of information in the world is increasing by over 60% per year! I shudder to myself, wondering what very small portion of all of this information we really, truly understand.

Luckily, there is a tool that can help simplify all of this information - the data model. A data model is a wayfinding tool for both business and IT professionals, which uses a set of symbols and text to precisely explain a subset of real information to improve communication within the organization and thereby lead to a more flexible and stable application environment. A line represents a motorway on a map of France. A box with the word 'Customer' within it represents the concept of a real Customer such as Bob, IBM, or Walmart on a data model.

In other words, a map simplifies a complex *geographic* landscape in the same way that a data model simplifies a complex *information* landscape. In many cases, the complexities in the actual data can make those roundabouts in France look ridiculously simple.

A data model is a set of symbols and text used for communicating a precise representation of an information landscape. There are many different forms available for describing the information landscape. Data models can look like the box and line drawings which are the subject of this book, or they can take other forms, such as Unified Modeling Language (UML) Class Diagrams, spreadsheets, or State Transition Diagrams. All of these models are wayfinding tools designed with the single purpose of simplifying complex information in our real world.

FUN WITH ICE CREAM

Perhaps the most common form of data model we work with on a daily basis is the spreadsheet. A spreadsheet is a representation of a paper worksheet, containing a grid defined by rows and columns, where each cell in the grid can contain text or numbers. The columns often contain different types of information. For example, I recently returned from a trip to Rome and I loved their ice cream (gelato). Upon entering a gelato store, you will see several spreadsheets. One example is shown in Table 1.1 which is a listing of ice cream. Table 1.2 contains the ice cream sizes along with prices (in Euros).

Banana
Cappuccino
Chocolate
Chocolate Chip
Coffee
Kiwi
Marshmallow
Pistachio
Strawberry
Vanilla

Table 1.1 Sample ice cream flavors

1 Scoop	1.75
2 Scoops	2.25
3 Scoops	2.60

Table 1.2 Ice cream sizes with prices

This is a data model because it is a set of symbols (in this case, text) that are used to describe something real in our world (in this case, the yummy ice cream flavors along with prices). Guess how many scoops of chocolate gelato I purchased?

The data model format that is the subject of this book is very similar to a spreadsheet. Although the definition of 'data model' is broader, going forward, when I use the term 'data model', I am referring to the format which is the subject of this book. Unlike a spreadsheet however, a data model:

- **Contains only types**. Data models don't usually display actual values such as `Chocolate` and `3 Scoops`. Data models display concepts or types. So a data model would display the type **Ice Cream Flavor** instead of showing the actual values `Chocolate` or `Vanilla`. A data model would display the type **Ice Cream Size** instead of showing the actual values `1 Scoop` or `2 Scoops`.

- **Contains interactions**. Data models capture how concepts interact with each other. For example, what is the interaction between **Ice Cream Flavor** and **Ice Cream Size**? If one orders three scoops, for example, must they all be the same flavor or could you have three different flavors? Interactions such as those between **Ice Cream Flavor** and **Ice Cream Size** are represented on a data model.

- **Provides a concise communication medium**. A single sheet of paper containing a data model communicates much more than a single piece of paper containing a spreadsheet. Data models display types and use simple yet powerful symbols to communicate interactions. We can capture all of the types and interactions within the ice cream example in a much more concise format using a data model rather than in a spreadsheet.

FUN WITH BUSINESS CARDS

Business cards contain a wealth of data about people and the companies for which they work. In this book, I illustrate many data modeling concepts by using business cards as the basis for a model. By building a business card data model, we see firsthand how much knowledge we gain from the actual values on a business card or, in a broader sense, the contact management area.

I opened the drawer in my nightstand (a scary proposition, as it had not been cleaned since the mid-1990s) and grabbed a handful of business cards. I laid them out and picked four that I thought would be the most fun to model. I chose my current business card, a business card from an internet business that my wife and I tried to start years ago, a business card from a magician who performed at one of our parties, and a business card from one of our favorite restaurants. I changed the names and contact information to protect the innocent, and reproduced them here, in Figure 1.2.

Figure 1.2 Four business cards from my nightstand

What information do you see on these business cards?

Assuming our objective with this exercise is to understand the information on the business cards, with an end goal of building a successful contact management application, let's begin by listing some of this information:

Steve Hoberman & Associates, LLC
BILL SMITH
Jon Smith
212-555-1212
MAGIC FOR ALL OCCASIONS
Steve and Jenn

58 Church Avenue
FINE FRESH SEAFOOD
President

We quickly realize that even though we are dealing with only four business cards, listing all the data would do little to aid our understanding. Now, imagine that instead of limiting ourselves to just these four cards, we looked through all the cards in my nightstand—or worse yet, every business card that has ever been received! We would become overloaded with data quickly.

A data model groups data together to make them easier to understand. For example, we would examine the following set of data and realize that they fit in a group (or spreadsheet column heading) called **Company Name**:

Steve Hoberman & Associates, LLC
The Amazing Rolando
findsonline.com
Raritan River Club

Another spreadsheet column heading could be **Phone Number**. Table 1.3 captures this subset of the business card information in the form of a spreadsheet.

	Company	**Phone number**
Business card 1	Steve Hoberman & Associates, LLC	212-555-1212
Business card 2	findsonline.com	(973) 555-1212
Business card 3	The Amazing Rolando	732-555-1212
Business card 4	Raritan River Club	(908) 333-1212 (908) 555-1212 554-1212

Table 1.3 Subset of business card information in a spreadsheet format

Taking this exercise a step further, we can organize the data on the cards into the following groups:

Person name
Person title
Company name

Email address
Web address
Mailing address
Phone number
Logo (the image on the card)
Specialties (such as "MAGIC FOR ALL OCCASIONS")

So, are we finished? Is this listing of groups a data model? Not yet. We are still missing a key ingredient: the interactions or relationships between these groups. For example, what is the interaction between **Company Name** and **Phone Number**? Can a **Company** have more than one **Phone Number**? Can a **Phone Number** belong to more than one **Company**? Can a **Company** exist without a **Phone Number**? These questions, and others, need to be asked and answered during the process of building the data model.

In order to build any wayfinding tool, one must get lost enough times to know the right path. For example, the first person who builds a map of a region must have taken quite a bit of time and made quite a few wrong turns before completing the map. The process of building a map is both challenging and time-consuming.

The same is true for the process of completing a data model. There is the 'data model' and then there is 'data modeling'. Data modeling is the process of building a data model. More specifically, data modeling is the set of techniques and activities that enable us to capture the structure and operations of an organization, as well as the proposed information solution that will enable the organization to achieve its goals. The process requires many skills, such as listening ability, courage to ask lots of questions, and even patience.

The data modeler needs to speak with individuals from many different departments with varying levels of technical and business experiences and skills. The data modeler not only needs to understand these individuals' views of their world, but also be able to demonstrate this understanding through feedback during the conversation and also as a final artifact in the form of the model. At the beginning of a project it is rare that you, as the data modeler, are handed all of the information you need to complete the model. It will require reading through lots of documentation and asking hundreds of business questions.

EXERCISE 1: EDUCATING YOUR NEIGHBOR

Reinforce your own understanding of what a data model is by explaining the concept of a data model to someone completely outside the world of IT, such as to a neighbor, family member or friend.

Did they get it?

Refer to the answers section at the back of the book to see how I explain the concept of a data model.

Key Points

✓ Wayfinding encompasses all of the techniques and tools used by people and animals to find their way from one site to another.

✓ A data model is a set of symbols and text used for communicating a precise representation of an information landscape.

✓ Data models come in many different forms. The most common and globally-understood form is a spreadsheet.

✓ The data model format that is the subject of this book is similar to the spreadsheet, yet is type-based, contains interactions, and is extensible.

✓ Data modeling is the process of building the data model. This process requires many non-technical skills, such as listening ability, courage to ask lots of questions, and patience.

Ambiguous talk
Data models are precise
Zero, one, many

Data modeling is an essential part of building an application. Communication and precision are the two key benefits that make a data model so important. This chapter explains these two core benefits, followed by a description of the areas within the business and application where the data model can be used. You will learn where communication occurs and about the three situations that can weaken data model precision.

COMMUNICATION

People with different backgrounds and levels of experience across departments and functional areas need to speak with each other about business concerns and to make business decisions. In a conversation, therefore, there is a need to know how the other party views concepts such as **Customer** or **Sales**. The data model is an ideal tool for understanding, documenting, and eventually reconciling different perspectives.

When the spoken word failed to reach me, the model that the gas station attendant drew for me clearly explained how to get to my destination. Regardless of whether we are trying to understand how key concepts in a business relate to one another or the workings of a 20-year-old order-processing system, the model becomes an ideal mechanism for explaining information.

Data models allow us to communicate the same information at different levels of detail. For example, I recently built a data model to capture consumer interactions within snack food. So if someone called up a company and complained about one of the company's products, the model I built would store this complaint and related information about it. The key business user and I built a very high-level data model showing the subjects that are relevant for the project. The model helped with scoping the project, understanding key terms such as **Consumer**, **Product**, and **Interaction**, and building a rapport with the business. Several months later, I used a much more detailed model of the same consumer-interaction information to inform the report developers of exactly what was expected to appear on each report along with all the necessary selection criteria.

The communication we derive from modeling does not begin when the data modeling phase has ended. That is, much communication and knowledge is shared during the process of building the model. The means are just as valuable as the end. Let's look at the communication benefits derived both during and after the modeling process in more detail.

COMMUNICATING DURING THE MODELING PROCESS

During the process of building data models, we are forced to analyze data and data relationships. We have no choice but to acquire a strong understanding of the content of what is being modeled. A lot of knowledge is gained as the people involved in the modeling process challenge each other about terminology, assumptions, rules, and concepts.

During the process of modeling a recipe management system for a large manufacturing company, I was amazed to witness team members with years of experience debate whether the concept of an **Ingredient** differed from the concept of **Raw Material**. After a 30 minute discussion on ingredients and raw materials, everyone who participated in this modeling effort benefited from the debate and left the modeling session with a stronger understanding of recipe management. When we model the business card example, you'll see that we can learn a lot about the person, company, and contact management in general, during the modeling process.

COMMUNICATING AFTER THE MODELING PROCESS

The completed data model is the basis for discussing what to build in an application, or more fundamentally, how something works. The data model becomes a reusable map to which analysts, modelers, and developers can refer to understand how things work. In much the same way as the first mapmaker painfully learned and documented a geographic landscape for others to use for navigation, the modeler goes through a similar exercise (often painful, but in a good way) so that others can understand an information landscape.

Before I started working at a large manufacturing company, my soon-to-be manager gave me a large book containing a set of data models for the company. I read this book several times, becoming familiar with the key concepts in the business and their business rules. On my first day on the job, I already knew alot about how the business worked. When my colleagues mentioned terms specific to the company, I already knew what they meant.

In our example with the business cards, once we complete the model, others can read it to learn about contact management.

PRECISION

Precision with respect to data modeling means that there is a clear, unambiguous way of reading every symbol and term on the model. You might argue with others about whether the rule is accurate, but that is a different argument. In other words, it is not possible for you to view a symbol on a model and say, "I see A here" and for someone else to view the same symbol and respond, "I see B here."

Going back to the business card example, let's assume we define a 'contact' to be the person or company that is listed on a business card. Someone states that *a contact has many phone numbers*. This statement is imprecise, as we do not know whether a contact can exist without a phone number, must have at least one phone number, or must have many phone numbers. Similarly, we do not know whether a phone number can exist without a contact, must belong to only one contact, or can belong to many contacts. The data model introduces precision, such as converting this vague statement into these assertions:

- Each contact must be reached by one or many phone numbers.
- Each phone number must belong to one contact.

Because the data model introduces precision, valuable time is not wasted trying to interpret the model. Instead, time can be spent debating and then validating the concepts on the data model.

There are three situations however, that can degrade the precision of a data model:

1. **Weak definitions**. If the definitions behind the terms on a data model are poor or nonexistent, multiple interpretations of terms become a strong possibility. Imagine a business rule on our model that states that an employee must have at least one benefits package. If the definition of **Employee** is something meaningless like "An **Employee** is a carbon-based life form", I may conclude that **Employee** includes **Job Applicants** and you may conclude that **Employee** does not include **Job Applicants**, and one of us will be wrong.

2. **Dummy data**. The second situation occurs when we introduce data that are outside the normal set of data values we would expect in a particular data grouping. An old fashioned trick for getting around the rigor of a data model is to expand the set of values that a data grouping can contain. For example, if a contact must have at least one phone number and for some reason, a contact arrives in the application with no phone numbers, one can create a fake phone number such as `Not Applicable` or `99` or `other` and then the contact can be entered. In this case, adding the dummy data allows a contact to exist without a phone number, which violates, but circumvents our original business rule.

3. **Vague or missing labels**. A model is read in much the same way as a book is read, with proper sentence structure. A very important part of the sentence is the verbs. On a data model, these verbs are captured when describing how concepts on the model relate to each other. Concepts like **Customer** and **Order** for example, may relate to each other through the verb 'place'. That is "A **Customer** may place one or many **Orders**." Vague verbs such as 'associate' or 'have', or missing verbs altogether, reduce the precision of the model, as we cannot accurately read the sentences.

In a data model, precision is also the result of applying a standard set of symbols. The traffic circles the gas station attendant drew for me were standard symbols that we both understood. There are also standard symbols used in data models, as we will discover shortly.

DATA MODEL USES

Traditionally, data models have been built during the analysis and design phases of a project to ensure the requirements for a new application are fully understood and correctly captured before the actual database is created. Due to being precise, the data model has additional uses as well:

- **To understand an existing application.** The data model provides a simple and precise picture of the concepts within an application. We can derive a data model from an existing application by examining the application's database and building a data model of its structures. The technical term for the process of building data models from existing applications is *reverse engineering*. Recently, a manufacturing organization needed to move a 25-year-old application to a new database platform. This was a very large application, so to understand its structures, we reverse engineered the database into a data model.

- **To manage risk.** A data model can capture the concepts and interactions that are impacted by a development project or program. What is the impact of adding or modifying structures for an application already in production? How many of an application's structures are needed for archival purposes? Many organizations today purchase software and then customize it. One example of managing risk through impact analysis would be to use data modeling to determine what impact modifying its structures would have on the purchased software.

- **To learn about the business.** As a prerequisite to a large development effort, it usually is necessary to understand how the business works before you can understand how the applications that support the business will work. For example, before building an order entry system, you need to understand the order entry business process.

One of my favorite sentences in the classic 1978 text *Data and Reality* by William Kent occurs during a section where Kent is discussing the steps required to build a database to store book information: *So, once again, if we are going to have a database about books, before we can know what one representative stands for, we had better have a consensus among all users as to what "one book" is.*

- **To educate team members.** When new team members need to come up to speed or developers need to understand requirements, a data model is an effective explanatory medium. Whenever a new person joined our department, I spent some time walking through a series of data models to educate the person on concepts as quickly as possible.

EXERCISE 2: CONVERTING THE NON-BELIEVER

Find someone in your organization who is a data model non-believer and try to convert him or her. What obstacles did you run into? Did you overcome them?

Key Points

- ✓ The two main benefits of a data model are communication and precision.

- ✓ Communication occurs both during the building of the data model and after its completion.

- ✓ Data model precision can be compromised by weak definitions, dummy data, and vague or missing labels.

- ✓ Communication and precision make a data model an excellent tool for building new applications.

- ✓ Other uses for data models include understanding existing applications and business areas, performing impact analysis, and educating team members.

What camera settings also apply to a data model?

Cameras have settings
Zoom, Focus, Timer, Filter
Data models, too

This chapter compares the data model to a camera, exploring four settings on the camera that equate perfectly to the data model. Understanding the impact these settings can have on a data model will increase the chances for a successful application. This chapter also compares the photograph's format to the three levels at which the data model can exist: conceptual, logical, and physical.

THE DATA MODEL AND THE CAMERA

A camera has many settings available to take the perfect picture. Imagine facing an awesome sunset with your camera. With the same exact sunset, you can capture a very different image based on the camera's settings, such as the focus, timer, and zoom. You might for example zoom out to capture as much of the sunset as possible, or zoom in and focus on people walking by with the sunset as a backdrop. It depends on what you want to capture in the photograph.

There are four settings on a camera that translate directly over to the data model: zoom, focus, timer, and filter. A model is characterized by one value from each setting. See Figure 3.1.

The zoom setting on the camera allows the photographer to capture a broad area with minimal detail, or a narrow scope but with more detail. Similarly, the scope setting for the model varies how much you see in the picture. The focus setting on the camera can make certain objects appear sharp or blurry. Similarly, the abstraction setting for the model can use generic concepts such as **Party** and **Event** to "blur" the distinction between concepts. The timer allows for a real-time snapshot or a snapshot for some time in the future. Similarly, the time setting for the model can capture a current view or a "to be" view sometime in the future. The filter setting can adjust the appearance of the entire picture to produce a certain effect. Similarly, the function setting for the model adjusts the model with either a business or application view.

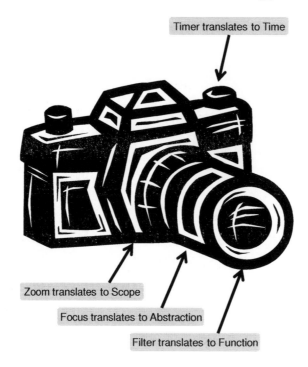

Figure 3.1 Camera settings that translate to data model variations

And don't forget that the type of photograph is important! A proof sheet shows all of the images on a single piece of paper, the negative has the raw format of the image, and the output can be in any one of a number of formats, including paper film, slide, or digital. Similarly, the same information image can exist at a conceptual, logical, or physical level of detail on a data model.

Which setting is right for your model? As with photographing the sunset, it depends on what you want to capture. Match the goals of your model with the appropriate model settings to improve the overall quality of the data model and the application it supports.

SCOPE

Both a data model and photograph have boundaries. Boundaries determine what will be shown. A photograph can capture my youngest daughter enjoying ice cream (actually her whole face enjoying the ice cream), or the photograph can capture my daughter and her surroundings, such as the ice cream shop. Similarly, the data model can include just claims processing, or it can include all concepts in the insurance business. Typically, the scope of a data model is a department, organization, or industry:

- **Department (Project)**. The most common type of modeling assignment has project-level scope. A project is a plan to complete a software development effort, often defined by a set of deliverables with due dates. Examples include a sales data mart, broker trading application, reservations system, and an enhancement to an existing application.

- **Organization (Program)**. A program is a large, centrally organized initiative that contains multiple projects. It has a start date and, if successful, no end date. Programs can be very complex and require long-term modeling assignments. Examples include a data warehouse, operational data store, and a customer relationship management system.

- **Industry.** An industry initiative is designed to capture everything in an industry, such as manufacturing or banking. There is much work underway in many industries to share a common data model. Industries such as health care and telecommunications have consortiums where common data modeling structures are being developed. Having such a common structure makes it quicker to build applications and easier to share information across organizations within the same industry.

ABSTRACTION

A photograph can be blurry or in focus. Similar to how the focus on a camera allows you to make the picture sharp or fuzzy, the abstraction setting for a model allows you to represent "sharp" (concrete) or "fuzzy" (generic) concepts.

Abstraction brings flexibility to your data models by redefining and combining some of the attributes, entities, and relationships within the model into more generic terms. Abstraction is the removal of details in such a way as to broaden applicability to a wider class of situations, while preserving the important properties and essential nature of concepts or subjects. By removing these details, we remove differences and change the way we view these concepts or subjects. We may now see similarities that were not apparent or even existent before. For example, we may abstract **Employee** and **Consumer** into the more generic concept of **Person**. A **Person** can play many **Roles**, two of which are **Employee** and **Consumer**. The more abstract a data model the fuzzier it becomes. On a data model, concepts can be represented at different levels of abstraction: 'in the business clouds', 'in the database clouds', or 'on the ground':

- **In the business clouds**. At this level of abstraction, only generic *business* terms are used on the model. The business clouds model hides much of the real complexity within generic concepts such as **Person**, **Transaction**, and **Document**. In fact, both a candy company and insurance company can look very similar to each other using business cloud concepts. If you lack business understanding or do not have access to business documentation and resources, a model 'in the business clouds' can work well.

- **In the database clouds**. At this level of abstraction, only generic *database (DB)* terms are used across the model. The database clouds model is the easiest level to create, as the modeler is "hiding" all of the business complexity within database concepts such as **Entity**, **Object**, and **Attribute**. If you have no idea how the business works and you want to cover all situations for all types of industries, a model 'in the database clouds' can work well.

- **On the ground**. This model uses a minimal amount of business and database cloud entities, with a majority of the concepts representing concrete business terms such as **Student**, **Course**, and **Instructor**. This model takes the most time to create of the three varieties. It also can add the most value towards understanding the business and resolving data issues.

TIME

Most cameras have a timer, allowing the photographer to run quickly and get in the picture. Similar to how the timer on a camera allows you to photograph a current or future scene, the time setting for a model allows you to represent a current or future "to be" view on a model.

A model can represent how a business works today or how a business might work sometime in the future:

- **Today**. A model with the today setting captures how the business works today. If there are archaic business rules, they will appear on this model, even if the business is planning on modifying them in the near future. In addition, if an organization is in the process of buying another company, selling a company, or changing lines of business, a today view would not show any of this. It would only capture an 'as is' view.

- **Tomorrow**. A model with the tomorrow setting can represent any time period in the future, and is usually an idealistic view. Whether end of the year, five years out, or 10 years out, a tomorrow setting represents where the organization wants to be. When a model needs to support an organization's vision or strategic view, a tomorrow setting is preferred. I worked on a university model that represented an end of year view, since that was when a large application migration would be completed. Note that most organizations who need a tomorrow view have to first build a today view to create a starting point. But that's ok! Just as a photographer can take more than one picture of a scene, so, too, can the data modeler build more than one data model with different setting values.

FUNCTION

Filters are plastic or glass covers that, when placed over the camera lens, adjust the picture with the color of the filter, such as making the picture more bluish or greenish. Similar to how a filter on a camera can change the appearance of a scene, the function setting for a model allows you to represent either a business or functional view on the model. Are we modeling the business' view of the world or the application's view of the world? Sometimes they can be the same and sometimes they may be very different:

- **Business**. This filter uses business terminology and rules. The model represents an application-independent view. It does not matter if the organization is using a filing cabinet to store its information, or the fastest software system out there; the information will be represented in business concepts.

- **Application**. This filter uses application terminology and rules. It is a view of the business through the eyes of an application. If the application uses the term 'Object' for the term 'Product', it will appear as 'Object' on the model and it will be defined according to the way the application defines the term, not how the business defines it.

FORMAT

A camera has a number of different formats in which the photo can be captured. The format setting adjusts the level of detail for a model, making the model either at a very broad and high level conceptual view, or a more detailed logical or physical view:

- **Conceptual**. Often when a set of photographs are developed, a proof sheet containing small thumbnail images of each photograph is included. The viewer can get a bird's eye view of all of the photographs on a single sheet of photo paper. This bird's eye view is analogous to the conceptual data model (CDM). A CDM represents the business at a very high level. It is a very broad view containing only the basic and critical concepts for a given scope. Here, basic means that the term is usually mentioned a hundred times a day in normal conversation. Critical means that without this term, the department, company, or industry would be greatly changed. Some terms are common to all organizations, such as **Customer**, **Product**, and **Employee**. Other terms are very industry or department specific, such as **Policy** for the insurance industry or **Trade** for the brokerage industry.

- **Logical**. Before the days of digital cameras, a roll of processed film would be returned with a set of negatives. These negatives represented a perfect view of the picture taken. The negative corresponds to the logical data model. A logical data model (LDM) represents a detailed business solution. It is how the modeler captures the business requirements without complicating the model with implementation concerns such as software and hardware.

- **Physical**. Although a negative is a perfect view of what was taken through the camera, it is not very practical to use. You can't, for example, put a negative in a picture frame or in a photo album and easily share it with friends. You need to convert or 'instantiate' the negative into a photograph or slide or digital image. Similarly, the logical data model usually needs to be modified to make it usable. Enter the physical data model (PDM), which is the 'incarnation' or 'instantiation' of the LDM, the same way as the photograph is the 'incarnation' of the negative. A PDM represents a detailed technology solution. It is optimized for a specific context (such as specific software or hardware). A physical data model is the logical data model modified with performance-enhancing techniques for the specific environment in which the data will be created, maintained, and accessed.

EXERCISE 3: CHOOSING THE RIGHT SETTING

In the following table, check off the most appropriate settings for each of these scenarios. When you are done, refer to the answers section at the back of the book.

1. Explain to a team of developers how an existing contact management application works

Scope	Abstraction	Time	Function
❑ Dept	❑ Bus clouds	❑ Today	❑ Bus
❑ Org	❑ DB clouds	❑ Tomorrow	❑ App
❑ Industry	❑ On the ground		

2. Explain the key manufacturing concepts to a new hire

Scope	Abstraction	Time	Function
❑ Dept	❑ Bus clouds	❑ Today	❑ Bus
❑ Org	❑ DB clouds	❑ Tomorrow	❑ App
❑ Industry	❑ On the ground		

3. Capture the detailed requirements for a new sales data mart (A data mart is a repository of data that is designed to meet the needs of a specific set of users)

Scope	Abstraction	Time	Function
❑ Dept	❑ Bus clouds	❑ Today	❑ Bus
❑ Org	❑ DB clouds	❑ Tomorrow	❑ App
❑ Industry	❑ On the ground		

Key Points

✓ There are four settings on a camera that translate directly to the model: zoom, focus, timer, and filter. Zoom translates into data model scope, focus into the level of abstraction, timer into whether the data model is capturing a current or future view, and filter into whether the model is capturing a business or application perspective.

✓ Match the goals of your model with the appropriate model settings to improve the overall quality of the data model and resulting application.

✓ Don't forget the photograph options! Would your audience prefer to view the proof sheet (conceptual data model), the negative (logical data model), or the photograph (physical data model)?

Section II explains all of the symbols and text on a data model. Chapter 4 explains entities, Chapter 5 is about attributes, Chapter 6 discusses relationships, and Chapter 7 is on keys. By the time you finish this section, you will be able to 'read' a data model of any size or complexity.

Chapter 4 defines an entity and discusses the different categories of entities. Entity instances are also defined. The three different levels at which entities may exist, conceptual, logical, and physical, are also explained, as well as the concepts of a weak verse strong entity.

Chapter 5 defines an attribute and discusses domains. Examples are provided for the three different types of domains.

Chapter 6 defines rules and relationships. Data rules are distinguished from action rules. Cardinality and labels are explained so that the reader can read any data model as easily as reading a book. Other types of relationships, such as recursive relationships, and subtyping are discussed, as well.

Chapter 7 defines keys and distinguishes the terms candidate, primary, alternate key. Surrogate keys and foreign keys are also defined, along with a discussion on their importance.

Concepts of interest
Who, What, When, Where, Why, and How
Entities abound

As I walked around the room to see if any students had questions, I noticed someone in the last row had already finished the exercise. I walked over to where she was sitting and noticed only a handful of boxes on the page. The large box in the center contained the word 'Manufacturing'. I asked her for her definition of 'Manufacturing'. "Manufacturing is the production process of how we turn raw materials into finished goods. All the manufacturing steps are in this box."

The data model boxes (also known as 'entities'), however, are not designed to represent or contain processes. Instead, they represent the concepts that are used *by* the processes. The **Manufacturing** entity on her model was eventually transformed into several other entities, including **Raw Material**, **Finished Goods**, **Machinery**, and **Production Schedule**.

This chapter defines the concept of an entity and discusses the different categories (Who, What, When, Where, Why and How) of entities. Entity instances are also defined. The three different levels of entities, conceptual, logical, and physical, are also explained, as well as the concepts of a weak versus a strong entity.

ENTITY EXPLAINED

An entity represents a collection of information about something that the business deems important and worthy of capture. Each entity is identified by a noun or noun phrase and fits into one of six categories: who, what, when, where, why, or how. Table 4.1 contains a definition of each of these entity categories along with examples.

Category	Definition	Examples
Who	Person or organization of interest to the enterprise. That is, "*Who* is important to the business?" Often a *Who* is associated with a role such as Customer or Vendor.	Employee, Patient, Player, Suspect, Customer, Vendor, Student, Passenger, Competitor, Author
What	Product or service of interest to the enterprise. It often refers to what the organization makes that keeps it in business. That is, "*What* is important to the business?"	Product, Service, Raw Material, Finished Good, Course, Song, Photograph, Title
When	Calendar or time interval of interest to the enterprise. That is, "*When* is the business in operation?"	Time, Date, Month, Quarter, Year, Semester, Fiscal Period, Minute
Where	Location of interest to the enterprise. Location can refer to actual places as well as electronic places. That is, "*Where* is business conducted?"	Mailing Address, Distribution Point, Website URL, IP Address
Why	Event or transaction of interest to the enterprise. These events keep the business afloat. That is, "*Why* is the business in business?"	Order, Return, Complaint, Withdrawal, Deposit, Compliment, Inquiry, Trade, Claim
How	Documentation of the event of interest to the enterprise. Documents record the events such as a Purchase Order recording an Order event. That is, "*How* does the business keep track of events?"	Invoice, Contract, Agreement, Purchase Order, Speeding Ticket, Packing Slip, Trade Confirmation

Table 4.1 Definitions and examples of entity categories

Entity instances are the occurrences or values of a particular entity. Think of a spreadsheet as being an entity where the column headings represent the pieces of information that may be recorded for each entity. Each spreadsheet row containing the actual values represents an entity instance. The entity **Customer** may have multiple customer instances with the names Bob, Joe, Jane, and so forth. The entity **Account** can have instances of Bob's checking account, Bob's savings account, Joe's brokerage account, and so on.

ENTITY TYPES

The beauty of data modeling is that you can take the same information and show it at different levels of detail depending on the audience. The previous chapter introduced the three levels of detail: conceptual, logical, and physical. Entities are components of all three levels.

Entities may be described at conceptual, logical, and physical levels of detail. The conceptual means the high level business solution to a business process or application effort frequently defining scope and important terminology, the logical means the detailed business solution to a business process or application effort, and the physical means the detailed technical solution to an application effort.

For an entity to be relevant at a conceptual level, it must be both basic and critical to the business. What is basic and critical depends very much on the scope. At a universal level, there are certain concepts common to most companies such as **Customer**, **Product**, and **Employee**. Making the scope slightly narrower, a given industry may have certain unique concepts. **Campaign**, for example, will be a valid concept for the advertising industry but perhaps not for all other industries.

Entities described at a logical level represent the business in more detail than at the conceptual level. Frequently, a conceptual entity represents many logical data model entities. Logical entities contain properties, often called "attributes," which we will discuss in Chapter 5.

At a physical level, the entities correspond to technology-specific objects such as database tables in a relational database management system (RDBMS) or collections in the NoSQL database MongoDB. The physical level is similar to the logical level but may include compromises that were needed to make up for deficiencies in technology, often related to performance or storage. The physical entities also contain database-specific information such as the format and length of an attribute (**Author Last Name** is 50 characters) and whether the attribute is required to have a value (**Author Tax Identifier** is not null and therefore required to have a value, but **Author Birth Date** is null and therefore not required to have a value).

In an RDBMS, these physical entities become database tables or views. In NoSQL databases, these physical entities become transformed depending on the underlying technology. For example, in MongoDB, a document-based database, these entities become collections. The general term "structure" will be used to refer to the underlying database components independent of whether the database is a RDBMS or NoSQL solution.

An entity is shown as a rectangle with its name inside. Figure 4.1 contains several entities from our gelato store.

Ice Cream Flavor

Ice Cream Size

Ice Cream Order

Figure 4.1 Sample entities

Notice that there are two types of rectangles: those with straight corners, such as **Ice Cream Flavor** and **Ice Cream Size**, and those with rounded edges, such as **Ice Cream Order**. Without introducing archaic data modeling jargon, it is enough to know that in most tools, the rectangles with straight right angle corners are strong and those with rounded corners are weak.

Strong entities stand on their own. They represent one occurrence of a person, place or thing independent of any other entities. In order to find the information about a particular **Customer**, for example, its **Customer Identifier** could be used to retrieve it from the database. "This is Bob, Customer Identifier 123." An **Ice Cream Flavor** of Chocolate might be retrieved with C. An **Ice Cream Size** of 2 Scoops might be retrieved with simply the number 2.

Weak entities need to rely on at least one other entity. This means you *cannot* retrieve an entity instance without referring to an entity instance from another entity. For example, **Ice Cream Order**, might be retrieved by an **Ice Cream Flavor** or **Ice Cream Size**, *in combination with* something within **Ice Cream Order** such as a **Sequence Number**.

A data model is a communication tool. Distinguishing strong from weak entities on the model helps us understand the relationships and dependencies between entities. For example, a developer reading a data model showing that **Ice Cream Order** is a weak entity that depends on **Ice Cream Flavor**, would develop the application program to ensure that an ice cream flavor is present before orders for it are placed. That is, Chocolate must be available as a flavor in the software system before an order for chocolate ice cream may be placed.

EXERCISE 4: DEFINING CONCEPTS

List three concepts in your organization. Does your organization have a single, agreed-upon definition for each of these terms? If not, why not? Can you achieve a single definition for each term?

Key Points

- ✓ An entity represents a collection of information about something that the business deems important and worthy of capture. An entity fits into one of several categories - who, what, when, where, why, or how.

- ✓ A noun or noun phrase identifies a specific entity.

- ✓ Entity instances are the occurrences or values of a particular entity.

- ✓ An entity can exist at the conceptual, logical, or physical level of detail.

- ✓ An entity can be strong or weak.

Spreadsheets have columns
Similar to attributes
Models all around

This chapter defines the concept of an attribute and the three different levels at which an attribute can exist: conceptual, logical, and physical. Domains and the different types of domains are also discussed.

ATTRIBUTE EXPLAINED

An attribute is an individual piece of information whose values identify, describe, or measure instances of an entity. The attribute **Claim Number** identifies each claim. The attribute **Student Last Name** describes the student. The attribute **Gross Sales Amount** measures the monetary value of a transaction.

Returning to our spreadsheet analogy, the column headings on a spreadsheet are attributes. The cells beneath each column heading are the values for that column heading. Attributes can be thought of as the column headings in a spreadsheet, the fields on a form, or the labels on a report. **Ice Cream Flavor Name** and **Ice Cream Size Code** are examples of attributes from our gelato store. **Company Name** and **Phone Number** are examples from the business card example.

ATTRIBUTE TYPES

As with entities, attributes can be described at conceptual, logical, and physical levels. An attribute at the conceptual level must be a concept both basic and critical to the business. We do not usually think of attributes as concepts, but depending on the business need, they can be. When I worked for a telecommunications company, **Phone Number** was an attribute that was so important to the business that it was represented on a number of conceptual data models.

An attribute on a logical data model represents a business property. Each attribute shown contributes to the business solution and is independent of any technology including software and hardware. For example, **Ice Cream Flavor Name** is a logical attribute because it has business significance regardless of whether records are kept in a paper file or within the fastest database out there. An attribute on a physical data model represents the physical "container" where the data is stored. The attribute **Ice Cream Flavor Name** might be represented as the column **ICE_CRM_FLVR_NAM** within the RDBMS table **ICE_CRM** or represented as the field name **IceCreamFlavorName** within the MongoDB collection **IceCream**.

I use the term *attribute* throughout the text for consistency. However, I would recommend using the term that is most comfortable for your audience. For example, a business analyst might prefer the term ''property' or 'label', while a database administrator might prefer the term 'column' or 'field'.

DOMAIN EXPLAINED

The complete set of all possible values that an attribute can be assigned is called a domain. A domain involves a set of validation criteria that can be applied to more than one attribute. For example, the domain **Date**, which contains all possible valid dates, can be assigned to any of these attributes:

- Employee Hire Date
- Order Entry Date
- Claim Submit Date
- Course Start Date

An attribute must never contain values outside of its assigned domain. The domain values are defined by specifying the actual list of values or a set of rules. **Employee Gender Code**, for example, may be limited to the domain of `female` and `male`. **Employee Hire Date** may initially be assigned the rule that its domain contain only valid dates, for example. Therefore, this may include values such as:

- February 15th, 2005
- 25 January 1910
- 20150410
- March 10th, 2050

Because **Employee Hire Date** is limited to valid dates, it does not include February 30th. An attribute may restrict a domain with additional rules. For example, by restricting the **Employee Hire Date** domain to dates earlier than today's date, we would eliminate March 10th, 2050. By restricting **Employee Hire Date** to YYYYMMDD (that is, year, month, and day concatenated), we would eliminate all the examples given except for 20150410. Another way of refining this set of values is to restrict the domain of **Employee Hire Date** to dates that fall on a Monday, Tuesday, Wednesday, Thursday, or Friday (that is, the typical workweek).

In our example of the business card, **Contact Name** may contain thousands or millions of values. The values from our four sample cards in Figure 1.2 would be

- Steve Hoberman
- Steve
- Jenn
- Bill Smith
- Jon Smith

This name domain may need a bit of refining. It may be necessary to clarify whether a valid domain value is composed of both a first and last name, such as Steve Hoberman, or just a first name, such as Steve. Could this domain contain company names such as IBM, as well? Could this domain contain numbers instead of just letters, such as the name R2D2 from the movie Star Wars? Could this domain contain special characters, such as the name O(+>?O(+>, representing "The Artist Formerly Known as Prince" (the musician Prince changed his name to this unpronounceable "Love Symbol" in 1993).

There are three basic domain types:

- **Format domains** specify the standard types of data one can have in a database. For example, Integer, Character(30), and Date are all format domains.

- **List domains** are similar to a drop-down list. They contain a finite set of values from which to choose. List domains are refinements of format domains. The format domain for **Order Status Code** might be Character(10). This domain can be further defined through a list domain of possible values {Open, Shipped, Closed, Returned}.

- **Range domains** allow all values that are between a minimum and maximum value. For example, **Order Delivery Date** must be between today's date and three months in the future. As with list domains, range domains are a refined version of a format domain.

Domains are very useful for a number of reasons:

- **Improves data quality by checking against a domain before inserting data**. This is the primary reason for having a domain. By limiting the possible values of an attribute, the chances of bad data getting into the database are reduced. For example, if every attribute that represents money is assigned the Amount domain, consisting of all decimal numbers up to 15 digits in length including two digits after the decimal point, then there is a good chance that each of these attributes actually do contain currency. **Gross Sales Amount,** which is assigned the amount domain, would not allow the value R2D2 to be added.

- **The data model communicates even more**. When we display domains on a data model, the data model communicates that a particular attribute has the properties of a particular domain and therefore, the data model becomes a more comprehensive communication tool. We learn, for example, that **Gross Sales Amount**, **Net Sales Amount**, and **List Price Amount** all share the Amount domain and therefore, share properties such that their valid values are limited to currency.

- **Greater efficiency in building new models and maintaining existing models.** When a data modeler embarks on a project, she can use a standard set of domains, thereby saving time by not reinventing the wheel. Any new attribute that ends in Amount, for example, would be associated with the standard Amount domain, saving analysis and design time.

EXERCISE 5: ASSIGNING DOMAINS

What is the most appropriate domain for each of the three attributes below?

- Email Address
- Gross Sales Amount
- Country Code

Key Points

✓ An attribute is a property of importance to the business whose values contribute to identifying, describing or measuring instances of an entity.

✓ A domain is a set of validation criteria that can be applied to more than one attribute.

✓ There are different types of domains, including format, list, and range domains.

Rules all around us
Relationships tell the tale
Connecting the dots

This chapter defines rules and relationships and the three different levels at which relationships can exist: conceptual, logical, and physical. Data rules are distinguished from action rules. Cardinality and labels are explained so that you can read any data model as easily as reading a book. Other types of relationships, such as recursive relationships and subtyping, are also discussed.

RELATIONSHIP EXPLAINED

In its most general sense, a rule is an instruction about how to behave in a specific situation. The following are examples of rules that you are familiar with:

- Your room must be cleaned before you can go outside and play.
- If you get three strikes, you are out and it is the next batter's turn.
- The speed limit is 55 miles per hour.

Rules are visually captured on our data model through relationships. A relationship is displayed as a line connecting two entities that captures the rule or navigation path between them. If the two entities are **Employee** and **Department**, the relationship can capture the rules "Each **Employee** must work for one **Department**" and "Each **Department** may contain one or many **Employees**."

RELATIONSHIP TYPES

A rule can be either a data rule or an action rule. Data rules are instructions on *how* data relate to one another. Action rules are instructions on *what to do* when attributes contain certain values. Let's talk about data rules first.

There are two types of data rules - structural and referential integrity (RI) data rules. Structural rules (also known as cardinality rules) define the quantity of each entity instance that can participate in a relationship. For example:

- Each product can appear on one or many order lines.
- Each order line must contain one and only one product.
- Each student must have a unique student number.

RI rules focus on ensuring valid values:

- An order line cannot exist without a valid product.
- A claim cannot exist without a valid policy.
- A student cannot exist without a valid student number.

When we define a structural rule, we get the corresponding RI rule for free. For example, if we define this structural rule on our data model, "Each order line must contain one and only one product", it is automatically assumed and included that "An order line cannot exist without a valid product."

Action rules on the other hand, are instructions on *what to do* when attributes contain certain values:

- Freshman students can register for at most 18 credits a semester.
- A policy must have at least three claims against it to be considered high-risk.
- Take 10% off of an order if the order contains more than five products.

In our data models, we can represent the data and enforce data rules, but we cannot enforce action rules on a data model. A student data model can capture the level of student, such as **Freshman** or **Senior**, as well as the number of credits each student is taking each semester, but cannot enforce that a freshman student register for no more than 18 credits a semester.

Returning to our ice cream example, I eventually ordered a double scoop of gelato in a cone - one scoop of Chocolate and one scoop of Banana. Many relationships can describe the process of placing this order, such as:

- An ice cream container may be either a cone or cup.
- Each ice cream container may contain many scoops of ice cream.
- Each ice cream scoop must reside in an ice cream container (or our hands would get really sticky holding that scoop of banana gelato).
- Each ice cream flavor may be chosen for one or many ice cream containers.
- Each ice cream container may contain many flavors.

The three levels of granularity (conceptual, logical, and physical) that apply to entities and attributes also apply to the relationships that connect entities. Conceptual relationships are high level rules or navigation paths that connect key concepts. Logical relationships are detailed business rules or navigation paths that enforce the rules between the logical entities. Physical relationships are detailed technology-dependent rules or navigation paths between the physical structures that the relationship connects. These physical relationships may eventually become database constraints in an RDBMS or references in a document-based database such as MongoDB.

CARDINALITY EXPLAINED

In a relationship between two entities, cardinality captures how many instances from one entity participate in the relationship with instances of the other entity. It is represented by the symbols that appear on each end of a relationship line. Cardinality specifies one kind of data rule that can be enforced. Without cardinality, the most we can say about a relationship is that two entities are connected in some way through a rule. For example, **Employee** and **Department** have some kind of relationship, but we may not know more than this. Note that the same two entities may be related in more than one way; for example each **Department** may contain one or many

Employees, but there could be a separate relationship capturing the **Employee** who manages that **Department**.

For cardinality, we can choose any combination of zero, one, or many. *Many* (some people read it as *more*) means any number greater than zero. Specifying zero or one allows us to capture whether or not an entity instance is *required* in a relationship. Specifying one or many allows us to capture *how many* of a particular instance participates in a given relationship.

Because our diagramming approach has only three cardinality symbols, we can't specify an exact number[1] (other than through documentation), as in "A **Car** contains four **Tires**." We can only say, "A **Car** may contain many **Tires**."

Each of the cardinality symbols is illustrated in the following example of **Ice Cream Flavor** and **Ice Cream Scoop**. An ice cream flavor is a selection for an ice cream scoop. An ice cream scoop must be one of the available ice cream flavors. Formalizing the rules between flavor and scoop, we have:

- Each **Ice Cream Flavor** may be the selection for one or many **Ice Cream Scoops**.
- Each **Ice Cream Scoop** must contain one **Ice Cream Flavor**.

Figure 6.1 captures these business rules.

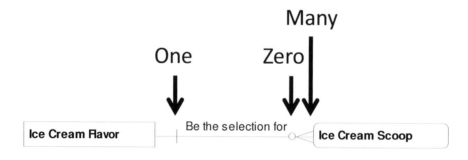

Figure 6.1 Ice Cream Flavor and Ice Cream Scoop, take 1

---

[1] Note that if you are using the Class Diagram in the Unified Modeling Language (UML for short), you can specify exact numbers in cardinality.

The small line means "one." The circle means "zero." The triangle with a line through the middle means "many." Some people call the "many" symbol a *crow's foot*. Relationship lines are frequently labeled to clarify the relationship and express the rule that the relationship represents. Thus, the label "Be the selection for" on the line in this example, helps in reading the relationship and understanding the rule.

Having a zero in the cardinality means we can use optional-sounding words such as 'may' or 'can' when reading the relationship. Without the zero, we use mandatory-sounding terms such as 'must' or 'have to'.

So instead of being redundant and saying:

- Each **Ice Cream Flavor** may be the selection for *zero*, one, or many **Ice Cream Scoops**.

We take out the word 'zero' because it can be expressed using the word 'may', which implies the zero:

- Each **Ice Cream Flavor** may be the selection for one or many **Ice Cream Scoops**.

A relationship has a parent and child. The parent entity appears on the "one" side of the relationship, and the child appears on the "many" side of the relationship. When I read a relationship, I always start with the entity on the one side of the relationship first. "Each **Ice Cream Flavor** may be the selection for one or many **Ice Cream Scoops**." It's then followed by reading the relationship from the many side: "Each **Ice Cream Scoop** must contain one **Ice Cream Flavor**." In truth, it doesn't matter which side you start from, as long as you are consistent.

I also always use the word 'each' in reading a relationship, starting with the parent side. The reason for the word 'each' is that you want to specify, on average how many instances of one entity relate to a different entity instance. 'Each' is a more user-friendly term to me than 'A'.

Let's change the cardinality slightly and see how this impacts the resulting business rule. Assume that because of the rough economy, this ice cream shop decides to allow consumers to select more than one flavor in a scoop. Figure 6.2 contains the updated cardinality.

Figure 6.2 Ice Cream Flavor and Ice Cream Scoop, take 2

This is known as a many-to-many relationship, in contrast to the previous example, which was a one-to-many relationship. The business rules here are read as follows:

- Each **Ice Cream Flavor** may be the selection for many **Ice Cream Scoops**.
- Each **Ice Cream Scoop** may contain many **Ice Cream Flavors**.

Make sure the labels on relationship lines are as descriptive as possible. Here are some examples of good label names:

- contain
- work for
- own
- initiate
- categorize
- apply to

Always avoid the following words as label names, as they provide no additional information to the reader (you can use these words in combination with other words to make a meaningful label name; just avoid using these words by themselves):

- has
- have
- associate
- participate
- relate
- be

For example, replace the relationship sentence:

A **Person** may be *associated with* one **Company**.

With:

A **Person** may be *employed by* one **Company**.

Many modelers capture labels on both sides of the relationship line, instead of just one side, as shown in this chapter. In weighing simplicity versus verbosity, I chose simplicity. The other label can be inferred from the label that appears on the model. For example, I assumed the label 'contain' in Figure 6.1 and read the rule from **Ice Cream Scoop** to **Ice Cream Flavor** this way: "Each **Ice Cream Scoop** must contain one **Ice Cream Flavor**."

RECURSION EXPLAINED

A recursive relationship is a rule that exists between instances of the same entity. A one-to-many recursive relationship describes a hierarchy, whereas a many-to-many relationship describes a network. In a hierarchy, an entity instance has at most one parent. In a network, an entity instance can have more than one parent. Let's illustrate both types of recursive relationships using **Employee**. See Figure 6.3 for a one-to-many recursive example and Figure 6.4 for a many-to-many example.

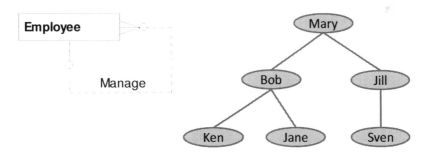

- Each **Employee** may manage one or many **Employees**.
- Each **Employee** may be managed by one **Employee**.

Figure 6.3 An Employee may work for one Manager

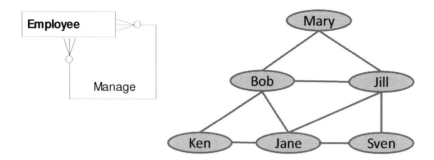

- Each **Employee** may manage one or many **Employees**.
- Each **Employee** may be managed by one or many **Employee**.

Figure 6.4 An Employee may work for many Managers

Using sample values such as Bob and Jill and sketching a hierarchy or network can really help understand, and therefore validate, cardinality. In Figure 6.3, for example, where the one-to-many captures a hierarchy, each employee has at most one manager. Yet in Figure 6.4 where the many-to-many captures a network, each employee must have many managers, such as Jane working for Bob, Jill, Ken, and Sven. (I would definitely update my resume if I were Jane.)

It is interesting to note that in both examples, there is optionality on both sides of the relationship. In this example, it implies we can have an **Employee** who has no boss (such as Mary) and an **Employee** who is not a manager (such as Jane).

Data modelers have a love-hate relationship with recursion. On the one hand, recursion makes modeling a complex business idea very easy and leads to a very flexible modeling structure. We can have any number of levels in an organization hierarchy in Figure 6.3, for example.

On the other hand, some consider using recursion to be taking the easy way out of a difficult modeling situation. There are many rules that can be obscured by recursion. For example, where is the **Regional Management Level** in Figure 6.4? It is hidden somewhere in the recursive relationship. Those in favor of recursion argue that you may not be aware of all the rules and that recursion protects you from having an incomplete model. The recursion adds a level of flexibility that ensures that any rules not previously considered are also handled by the model. It is therefore wise to consider recursion on a case-by-case basis, weighing obscurity against flexibility.

SUBTYPING EXPLAINED

Subtyping allows grouping the common attributes and relationships of similar or related entities. Subtyping is an excellent way of communicating that certain concepts are very similar and for showing examples.

In our ice cream example, we are told that an ice cream cone and ice cream cup can each contain many scoops of ice cream, as illustrated in Figure 6.5.

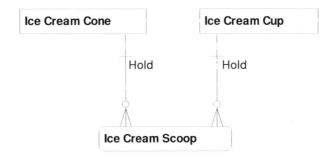

- Each **Ice Cream Cone** may hold one or many **Ice Cream Scoops**.
- Each **Ice Cream Scoop** must be held in one **Ice Cream Cone**.
- Each **Ice Cream Cup** may hold one or many **Ice Cream Scoops**.
- Each **Ice Cream Scoop** must be held in one **Ice Cream Cup**.

Figure 6.5 Ice cream example before subtyping

Rather than repeat the relationship to **Ice Cream Scoop** twice, we can introduce subtyping, as shown in Figure 6.6.

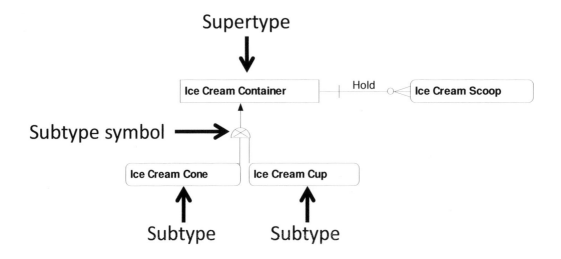

- Each **Ice Cream Container** may hold one or many **Ice Cream Scoops**.
- Each **Ice Cream Scoop** must be held in one **Ice Cream Container**.
- Each **Ice Cream Container** may be either an **Ice Cream Cone** or an **Ice Cream Cup**.
- Each **Ice Cream Cone** is an **Ice Cream Container**.
- Each **Ice Cream Cup** is an **Ice Cream Container**.

Figure 6.6 Ice cream example after subtyping

The subtyping relationship implies that all of the properties from the supertype are inherited by the subtype. Therefore, there is an implied relationship from **Ice Cream Cone** to **Ice Cream Scoop** as well as **Ice Cream Cup** to **Ice Cream Scoop**. Not only does subtyping reduce redundancy on a data model, it makes it easier to communicate similarities across what otherwise would appear to be distinct and separate concepts.

EXERCISE 6: READING A MODEL

Practice reading the relationships in this model. When you are done, refer to the answers section at the back of the book.

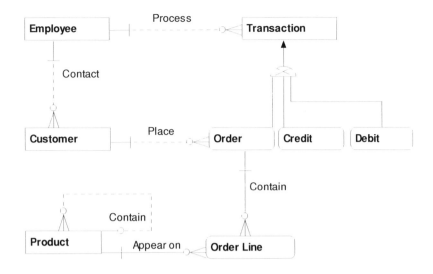

Key Points

✓ A rule is visually captured on a data model by a line connecting two entities, called a relationship.

✓ Data rules are instructions on *how* data relate to one another. Action rules are instructions on *what to do* when attributes contain certain values.

✓ Cardinality is represented by the symbols on both ends of a relationship that define the number of instances of each entity that can participate in the relationship. The three simple choices are zero, one, or many.

✓ Labels are the verbs that appear on the relationship lines. Labels should be as descriptive as possible to retain data model precision.

✓ A recursive relationship is a rule that exists between instances of the same entity.

✓ Subtyping allows grouping the common attributes and relationships of similar or related entities.

CHAPTER 7
What are keys?

More than one John Doe
Which is the right Customer?
Recall by the key

There is a lot of data out there, but how do you sift through it all to find what you're looking for? That's where keys come in. A key is one or more attributes whose purposes include enforcing rules, efficiently retrieving data, and allowing navigation from one entity to another. This chapter defines keys and distinguishes between the terms candidate, primary, and alternate keys. Surrogate keys and foreign keys and their importance are also explained.

CANDIDATE KEY (PRIMARY AND ALTERNATE) EXPLAINED

A candidate key is one or more attributes that uniquely identify an entity instance. An **ISBN** (International Standard Book Number) is assigned to every title. The **ISBN** uniquely identifies each title and is therefore the title's candidate key. When the **ISBN** for this title, 9780977140060, is entered into many search engines and database systems, the book entity instance Data Modeling Made Simple will be returned (try it!). **Tax ID** can be a candidate key for an organization in some countries such as the United States. **Account Code** can be a candidate key for an account. A **VIN** (Vehicle Identification Number) identifies a vehicle.

Sometimes a single attribute identifies an entity instance such as **ISBN** for a title. Sometimes it takes more than one attribute to uniquely identify an entity instance. For example, both a **Promotion Type Code** and **Promotion Start Date** may be necessary to identify a promotion. When more than one attribute makes up a key, we use the term *composite key*. Therefore, **Promotion Type Code** and **Promotion Start Date** together are a composite candidate key for a promotion.

A candidate key has four main characteristics:

- **Unique**. A candidate key value must not identify more than one entity instance (or one real-world thing).

- **Mandatory**. A candidate key may not be empty (also known as *nullable*). Each entity instance must be identified by exactly one candidate key value. Therefore, the number of distinct values of a candidate key is always equal to the number of distinct entity instances. If the entity **Title** has **ISBN** as its candidate key, and if there are 500 title instances, there will also be 500 unique ISBNs.

- **Non-volatile**. A candidate key value on an entity instance should never change.

- **Minimal**. A candidate key should contain only those attributes that are needed to uniquely identify an entity instance. If four attributes are listed as the composite candidate key for an entity, but only three are really needed for uniqueness, then only those three should make up the candidate key.

For example, each **Student** may attend one or many **Classes**, and each **Class** may contain one or many **Students**. Table 7.1 contains sample instances for each of these entities.

Student

Student Number	First Name	Last Name	Birth Date
SM385932	Steve	Martin	1/25/1958
EM584926	Eddie	Murphy	3/15/1971
HW742615	Henry	Winkler	2/14/1984
MM481526	Mickey	Mouse	5/10/1982
DD857111	Donald	Duck	5/10/1982
MM573483	Minnie	Mouse	4/1/1986
LR731511	Lone	Ranger	10/21/1949
EM876253	Eddie	Murphy	7/1/1992

Attendance

Attendance Date
5/10/2015
6/10/2015
7/10/2015

Class

Class Full Name	Class Short Name	Class Description Text
Data Modeling Fundamentals	Data Modeling 101	An introductory class covering basic data modeling concepts and principles.
Advanced Data Modeling	Data Modeling 301	A fast-paced class covering techniques such as advanced normalization and ragged hierarchies.
Tennis Basics	Tennis One	For those new to the game of tennis; learn the key aspects of the game.
Juggling		Learn how to keep three balls in the air at once!

Table 7.1 Sample values for Student

Based on our definition of a candidate key (and a candidate key's characteristics of being unique, stable, mandatory, and minimal) what would you choose as the candidate keys for each of these entities?

For **Student**, **Student Number** appears to be a valid candidate key. There are eight students and eight distinct values for **Student Number**. So unlike **Student First Name** and **Student Last Name**, which can contain duplicates like `Eddie Murphy`, **Student Number** appears to be unique. **Student Birth Date** can also contain duplicates such as `5/10/1982`, which is the **Student Birth Date** for both `Mickey Mouse` and `Donald Duck`. The combination of **Student First Name**, **Student Last Name**, and **Student Birth Date** may be a valid composite candidate key.

For **Attendance**, we are currently missing a candidate key. Although the **Attendance Date** is unique in this sample data, we will probably need to know which student attended which class on this particular date, so this definition of **Attendance** is inadequate.

For **Class**, on first glance it appears that any of its attributes are unique and would therefore qualify as a candidate key. However, `Juggling` does not have a **Class Short Name**. Therefore, because **Class Short Name** can be empty, we cannot consider it a candidate key. In addition, one of the characteristics of a candidate key is that it is non-volatile. I know, based on my teaching experience, that class descriptions can change. Therefore, **Class Description Text** also needs to be ruled out as a candidate key, leaving **Class Full Name** as the best option for a candidate key. Even though an entity may contain more than one candidate key, we can only select one candidate key to be the primary key for an entity. A primary key is the candidate key that has been chosen to be *the preferred* unique identifier for an entity. An alternate key is a candidate key that, although it has the properties of being unique, stable, mandatory, and minimal, was not chosen as the primary key though it may still be used to find specific entity instances.

We have only one candidate key in the **Class** entity, so **Class Full Name** becomes our primary key. We have to make a choice in **Student**, however, because we have two candidate keys. Which **Student** candidate key would you choose as the primary key?

In selecting one candidate key over another as the primary key, consider succinctness and privacy. Succinctness means if there are several candidate keys, choose the one with the fewest attributes or shortest in length. In terms of privacy, it is possible that one or more attributes within a candidate key will contain sensitive data whose viewing should be restricted. We want to avoid having sensitive data in our entity's primary key because the primary key can propagate as a foreign key and therefore spread this sensitive data throughout our database.

Considering succinctness and security in our example, I would choose **Student Number** over the composite **Student First Name**, **Student Last Name**, and **Student Birth Date**. It is more succinct and contains less sensitive data. Figure 7.1 contains our data model with primary and alternate keys.

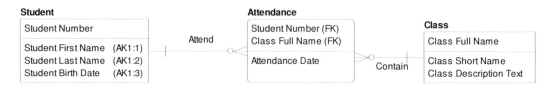

Figure 7.1 Data model updated with primary and alternate keys

Primary key attributes are shown above the line in the rectangles. You will notice two numbers following the key abbreviation "AK." The first number is the grouping number for an alternate key, and the second number is the ordering of the attribute within the alternate key. So there are three attributes required for the **Student** alternate key: **Student First Name**, **Student Last Name**, and **Student Birth Date**. This is also the order in which the alternate key index will be created because **Student First Name** has a "1" after the colon, **Student Last Name** a "2", and **Student Birth Date** a "3."

Attendance now has as its primary key **Student Number** and **Class Full Name**, which appear to make a valid primary key. Note that the two primary key attributes of **Attendance** are followed by "FK". These are foreign keys, to be discussed shortly.

So to summarize, a candidate key consists of one or more attributes that uniquely identify an entity instance. The candidate key that is determined to be the best way to identify each record in the entity becomes the primary key. The other candidate keys become alternate keys. Keys containing more than one attribute are known as composite keys.

At the physical level, a candidate key is often translated into a unique index.

SURROGATE KEY EXPLAINED

A surrogate key is a unique identifier for a table, often a counter, usually fixed-size, and always system-generated without intelligence, so a surrogate key carries no business meaning. (In other words, you can't look at a month identifier of 1 and assume that it represents the **Month** entity instance value of January.) Surrogate keys should not be visible to the business but should remain behind the scenes to allow for more efficient navigation across structures and to facilitate integration across applications.

Surrogate keys are also efficient. You've seen that a primary key may be composed of one or more attributes of the entity. A single surrogate key is more efficient to use than having to specify three or four (or five or six) attributes to locate the single record you're looking for. Surrogate keys are useful for integration, which is an effort to create a single, consistent version of the data.

When using a surrogate key, always make an effort to determine the natural key, which is what the business would consider to be the way to uniquely identify the entity, and then define this natural key as an alternate key. For example, assuming a surrogate key is a more efficient primary key than **Class Full Name**, we can create the surrogate key **Class ID** for **Class** and define an alternate key on the natural key **Class Full Name**, as shown in Figure 7.2 along with the values in **Class**.

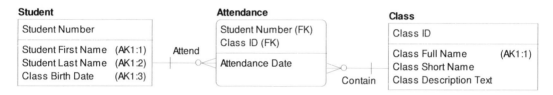

Class ID	Class Full Name	Class Short Name	Class Description Text
1	Data Modeling Fundamentals	Data Modeling 101	An introductory class covering basic data modeling concepts and principles.
2	Advanced Data Modeling	Data Modeling 301	A fast-paced class covering techniques such as advanced normalization and ragged hierarchies.
3	Tennis Basics	Tennis One	For those new to the game of tennis; learn the key aspects of the game.
4	Juggling		Learn how to keep three balls in the air at once!

Figure 7.2 Data model updated with surrogate key

FOREIGN KEY EXPLAINED

The entity on the "one" side of the relationship is called the parent entity, and the entity on the "many" side of the relationship is called the child entity.

When we create a relationship from a parent entity to a child entity, the primary key of the parent is copied as a foreign key to the child.

A foreign key is one or more attributes that provide a link to another entity (or in a case of a recursive relationship where two instances of the same entity may be related, a link to the same entity). At the physical level, a foreign key allows a relational database management system to navigate from one table to another. For example, if we need to know the customer who owns an account, we would want to include the **Customer ID** in the **Account** entity. The **Customer ID** in **Account** is the primary key for **Customer**.

Using this foreign key back to **Customer** enables the database management system to navigate from a particular account or accounts to the customer or customers that own each account. Likewise, the database can navigate from a particular customer or customers to find all of their accounts. Our data modeling tools automatically create a foreign key when a relationship is defined between two entities.

In our **Student/Class** model, there are two foreign keys in **Attendance**. The **Student Number** foreign key points back to a particular student in the **Student** entity, and the **Class ID** foreign key points back to a particular **Class** in the **Class** entity, as shown in Table 7.2.

Student Number	Class ID	Attendance Date
SM385932	1	5/10/2015
EM584926	1	5/10/2015
EM584926	2	6/10/2015
MM481526	2	6/10/2015
MM573483	2	6/10/2015
LR731511	3	7/10/2015

Table 7.2 Attendance entity instances

SECONDARY KEY EXPLAINED

Sometimes there is a need to retrieve data rapidly from a table to answer a business query or meet a certain response time. A secondary key is one or more attributes (if there is more than one attribute, it is called a composite secondary key) that are accessed frequently and need to be retrieved quickly. A secondary key is also known as a non-unique index or inversion entry (IE for short). A secondary key does not have to be unique, stable, nor always contain a value. For example, we can add a secondary key to **Student Last Name** in **Student** to allow for quick retrieval whenever any queries require **Student Last Name**. See Figure 7.3.

Figure 7.3 Data model updated with secondary key

Student Last Name is not unique, as there can be two `Murphys`; it is not stable and can change over time; and although it may be rare, there could be times when we may not know someone's last name, so it can be empty.

EXERCISE 7: CLARIFYING CUSTOMER ID

I was showing examples of both complete and incomplete definitions during a recent training class, when I shared the following incomplete definition for a **Customer Id**:

*A **Customer Id** is the unique identifier for a Customer.*

"What else can you say about **Customer Id** anyway?" a participant asked.

What else can you say about **Customer Id** (or any identifier) to add more meaning to its definition?

When you are done, refer to the answers section at the back of the book.

Key Points

- ✓ A key is one or more attributes whose purposes include enforcing rules, efficiently retrieving data, and allowing navigation from one entity to another.

- ✓ A candidate key is one or more attributes that uniquely identify an entity instance.

- ✓ A primary key is the candidate key that has been chosen to be *the preferred* unique identifier for an entity. An alternate key is a candidate key that, although it has the properties of being unique, stable, and minimal, was not chosen as the primary key though it may still be used to find specific entity instances.

- ✓ If a key contains more than one attribute, it is known as a composite key.

- ✓ A surrogate key is a primary key with no embedded intelligence that is a substitute for a natural key. It is used by IT to facilitate integration and introduce database efficiencies.

- ✓ A foreign key is one or more attributes that provide a link to another entity (or in a case of a recursive relationship, where two instances of the same entity may be related, a link to the same entity).

- ✓ A secondary key is one or more attributes (if there is more than one attribute, it is called a composite secondary key) that are accessed frequently and need to be retrieved quickly.

Section III explores the three different levels of models: conceptual, logical, and physical. A conceptual data model (CDM) represents the business need within a defined scope, a logical data model (LDM) the detailed business solution, and a physical data model (PDM) the detailed technical solution. Chapter 8 focuses on the CDM, Chapter 9 the LDM, and Chapter 10 the PDM.

In addition to these three levels of detail, there are also two different modeling mindsets: relational and dimensional. Relational data modeling is the process of capturing how the business *works* by precisely representing business rules, while dimensional data modeling is the process of capturing how the business is *monitored* by precisely representing navigation.

The major difference between relational and dimensional data models is in the meaning of the relationship lines. On a relational data model a relationship communicates a business rule, and on dimensional data model a relationship communicates a navigation path. On a relational data model, for example, we can represent the business rule "A **Customer** must have at least one **Account**." On a dimensional data model we can display the measure **Gross**

Sales Amount along with all of the navigation paths that a user needs to see **Gross Sales Amount** at, such as by day, month, year, region, account, and customer. The dimensional data model is all about viewing measures at different levels of granularity.

The following table summarizes these three levels of detail and two modeling mindsets, leading to five different types of models:

		Mindset	
		Relational	**Dimensional**
Types of models	**CDM**	Key concepts and their business rules, such as a "Each Customer may place one or many Orders."	Key concepts focused around one or more measures, such as "I want to see Gross Sales Amount by Customer."
	LDM	All attributes required for a given application or business process, neatly organized into entities according to strict business rules and independent of technology such as "Each Customer ID value must return at most one Customer Last Name."	All attributes required for a given reporting application, focused on measures and independent of technology such as "I want to see Gross Sales Amount by Customer and view the customer's first and last name."
	PDM	The LDM modified for a specific technology such as database or access software. For example, "To improve retrieval speed, we need a non-unique index on Customer Last Name." Or "To improve retrieval speed, we need to embed this MongoDB collection within that MongoDB collection."	

Each of these five models will be explained in detail in this section. Chapter 8 goes into detail on the conceptual data model, discussing the variations along with how to build this type of model. Chapter 9 focuses on the relational and dimensional logical data model. Chapter 10 focuses on the physical data model, going through the different techniques for building an effective design, such as denormalization and partitioning. Slowly Changing Dimensions (SCDs) are also discussed in this chapter.

Need the Big Picture?
No common definitions?
Build a CDM!

The highlighted row in Table 8.1 shows the focus of this chapter: the conceptual data model (CDM).

	Relational	Dimensional
Conceptual Data Model (CDM)	**"One-pager" on business rules**	**"One-pager" on navigation**
Logical Data Model (LDM)	Detailed business solution on business rules	Detailed business solution on navigation
Physical Data Model (PDM)	Detailed technical solution	

Table 8.1 The Conceptual Data Model is the focus of this chapter

A CDM shows the key concepts in a particular area and how these concepts interact with each other. This chapter defines a concept, followed by an explanation of the importance of the conceptual data model and concept definitions. Then both relational and dimensional CDMs will be discussed. Then we provide a summary of the five-step approach to building a conceptual data model.

CONCEPT EXPLAINED

A concept is a key idea that is both *basic* and *critical* to your audience. "Basic" means this term is probably mentioned many times a day in conversations with the people who are the audience for the model. "Critical" means the business would be very different or non-existent without this concept.

The majority of concepts are easy to identify and include ideas that are common across industries, such as **Customer**, **Employee**, and **Product**. An airline may call a **Customer** a **Passenger**, and a hospital may call a **Customer** a **Patient**, but in general they are all people who receive goods or services. Each concept will be shown in much more detail at the logical and physical phases of design. For example, the **Customer** concept might encompass the logical entities **Customer**, **Customer Association**, **Customer Demographics**, **Customer Type**, and so on.

Many concepts, however, can be more challenging to identify, as they may be concepts to your audience but not to others in the same department, company, or industry. For example, **Account** would most likely be a concept for a bank and for a manufacturing company. However, the audience for the bank conceptual data model might also require **Checking Account** and **Savings Account** to be on their model, whereas the audience for the manufacturing conceptual data model might, instead, require **General Ledger Account** and **Accounts Receivable Account** to be on the model.

In our example with the business card, a basic and critical concept can be **Address**, but **Mailing Address** can also be basic and critical. Should the conceptual data model for contact management contain **Mailing Address** as well? To answer this question, we need to know whether **Mailing Address** is basic and critical to your audience.

CONCEPTUAL DATA MODEL EXPLAINED

Concepts such as those in the preceding discussion are represented on a conceptual data model. A conceptual data model is a one-page data model that captures the business need and project scope, designed for a particular audience. Limiting the conceptual data model to one page is important because it forces the modeler and participants to select only key concepts. We can fit 20 concepts on one page but not 500 concepts. A good rule of thumb, therefore, is to ask yourself if the audience for this model would include this concept as one of the top 20 concepts in their business. This will rule out concepts that are at too low a level of detail; they will appear in the more detailed logical data model. If you're having trouble limiting the number of concepts, think about whether or not there are other concepts into which the ones you're discussing could be grouped, such as grouping **Order Line** into **Order**. These higher concepts are the ones you should be including in the conceptual data model.

The conceptual data model includes concepts, their definitions, and the relationships that show how these concepts interact with each other. Unlike the logical and physical data models, as we will see, conceptual data models may contain many-to-many relationships. A sample conceptual data model appears in Figure 8.1.

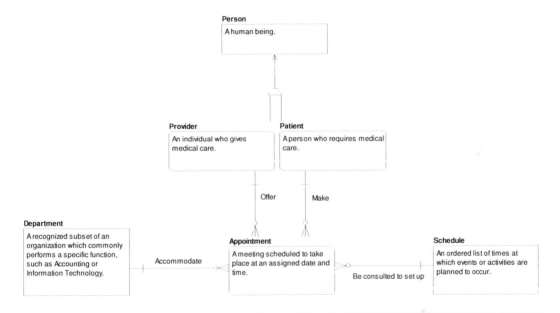

Figure 8.1 Healthcare Facility Appointment Conceptual Data Model

Business Rules (listed in the order we would typically walk someone through the model):

- Each **Person** may be a **Provider**, a **Patient**, or both a **Provider** and a **Patient**. Note that when the subtyping symbol does *not* have an 'X' in its center (as shown in Figure 8.1), it indicates that a member of the supertype can play more than one subtype role. This is called an inclusive (overlapping) subtype. Here, a particular person can be both a provider and a patient.
- Each **Provider** is a **Person**.

- Each **Patient** is a **Person**.
- Each **Provider** may offer one or many **Appointments**.
- Each **Patient** may make one or many **Appointments**.
- Each **Schedule** may be consulted to set up one or many **Appointments**.
- Each **Department** may accommodate one or many **Appointments**.
- Each **Appointment** must involve one **Provider**, one **Patient**, one **Department**, and one **Schedule**.

Notice on the model in Figure 8.1 that concepts such as **Provider** and **Patient** are likely to be considered concepts throughout the healthcare industry. There are also slightly more detailed concepts on this model, such as **Schedule** and **Appointment**, which are considered basic and critical and are therefore concepts for the particular audience for this conceptual data model. Yet these more detailed concepts may not be considered concepts within a different department, such as accounting and marketing, in this same healthcare company.

During the conceptual data modeling phase, documenting clearly and completely what each concept means is critical. All too often, we wait until it is too late in the development process to get definitions. Waiting too long usually leads to not writing definitions at all or doing a rush job by writing quick definition phrases that have little or no usefulness. If the definitions behind the terms on a data model are nonexistent or poor, multiple interpretations of the concept become a strong possibility, as discussed earlier.

By agreeing on definitions at the concept level, the more detailed logical and physical analysis will go smoother and take less time. For example, definitions can address the question, "Does Customer include potential customers or only existing customers?" See the cartoon in Figure 8.2 for an example of what not to do.

We need to do a better job of capturing definitions. In fact, during a recent presentation to over 100 business analysts, I asked the innocent question, "How many of you have an agreed-upon single definition of **Customer** in your organization?" I was expecting at least a handful of the 100 participants to raise their hands, but no one in the room raised their hand!

Figure 8.2 Clarify key concept definitions early!

There are three main reasons why definitions are important:

- **Assists business and IT with decision making**. If a business user has a different interpretation of a concept than what was actually implemented, it is easy for poor decisions to be made, compromising the entire application. If a business user would like to know how many products were ordered each month, for example, imagine the poor judgments that could result if the user expected raw materials to be included with products and they were not. Or, what if he or she assumed that raw materials were not included, but they were?

- **Helps initiate, document and resolve different perspectives on the same concept**. The CDM is a great medium for resolving differences in opinion on the meaning of high-level terms. Folks in accounting and sales can both agree that **Customer** is an important concept. But can both groups agree on a common definition? If they can agree, you are one step closer to creating a holistic view of the business.

- **Supports data model precision**. A data model is precise. This assumes that the concept definitions are also precise. An **Order Line** cannot exist without a **Product**, for example. However, if the definition of **Product** is missing or vague, we have less confidence in the concept and its relationships. Is a **Product**, for example, raw materials and intermediate goods, or only a finished item ready for resale? Can we have an order for a service, or must a product be a tangible deliverable? The definition is needed to support the **Product** concept and its relationship to **Order Line**.

When the conceptual data model is complete, which includes concept definitions, it is a powerful tool that can provide a number of important business benefits:

- **Provides broad understanding**. We can capture extremely complex and encompassing business processes, application requirements, and even entire industries on a single piece of paper. This enables people with different backgrounds and roles to understand and communicate with each other on the same concepts, agreeing or debating on issues.

- **Defines scope and direction**. By visually showing concepts and their business rules, we can more easily identify a subset of the model to analyze. For example, we can model the entire logistics department, and then scope out of this a particular logistics application that we would like to build. The broad perspective of a conceptual data model can help us determine how planned and existing applications will coexist. It can provide direction and guidance on what new functionality the business will need next.

- **Offers proactive analysis**. By developing a conceptual understanding of the application, there is a strong chance we will be able to identify important issues or concerns, saving substantial time and money later on. Examples include concept definition differences and different interpretations on project scope.

- **Builds rapport between IT and the business**. A majority of organizations have some level of internal communication issues between the business and IT departments. Building a conceptual data model together is a great way to remove or reduce these communication barriers. On one occasion, a key business user and I sketched out a

Contact Data Mart conceptual data model, which built not just business understanding, but also a strong relationship with this key user.

RELATIONAL AND DIMENSIONAL CONCEPTUAL DATA MODELS

Recall from this section's introduction that relational data modeling is the process of capturing how the business *works* by precisely representing business rules, while dimensional data modeling is the process of capturing how the business is *monitored* by precisely representing navigation. There are both relational and dimensional conceptual data models.

RELATIONAL CDM EXAMPLE

The relational conceptual model includes concepts, their definitions, and the relationships that capture the business rules binding these concepts. Unlike the logical and physical data models, as we will see, conceptual models may contain many-to-many relationships. For example, Figure 8.3 contains part of a financial relational CDM.

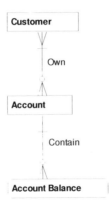

Figure 8.3 Financial relational CDM subset

Following is a full list of the concept definitions we arrived at from our meetings with the project sponsor:

Customer	A customer is a person or organization who obtains our product for resale. A person or organization must have obtained at least one product from us to be considered a customer. That is, prospects are not customers. Also, once a customer, always a customer, so even customers that have not obtained anything in 50 years are still considered customers. The customer is different than the consumer, who purchases the product for consumption as opposed to resale.
Account	An account is a contractual arrangement by which our bank holds funds on behalf of a customer.
Account Balance	An account balance is a financial record of how much money a customer has with our bank at the end of a given time period such as someone's checking account balance at the end of a month.

Business Rules (listed in the order we would typically walk someone through the model):

- Each **Customer** may own one or many **Accounts**.
- Each **Account** must be owned by one or many **Customers**.
- Each **Account** may contain one or many **Account Balances**.
- Each **Account Balance** must belong to one **Account**.

Notice that in this example definitions were not displayed directly on the diagram as on the model in Figure 8.1. I find that if the data model is small enough (and the definitions are short enough), it can be a valuable communication tool to display the definitions on the diagram. I also choose to display the definitions when I need to highlight poor or lacking definitions or definitions that I know will spur debate.

DIMENSIONAL CDM EXAMPLE

To understand and document our reporting requirements, we can also build a dimensional CDM such as the example in Figure 8.4.

In this case, we'd like to see certain measures around account balances (such as **Account Balance Amount**) at a **Region, Account,** and **Month** level and then have the ability to navigate to higher levels (e.g., viewing **Account Balance Amount** at a **Country** level). We take measures such as **Account Balance Amount** up and down hierarchies. A hierarchy is when an entity instance is a child of at most one other entity instance such as the month `January 2016` belonging to only the year `2016`.

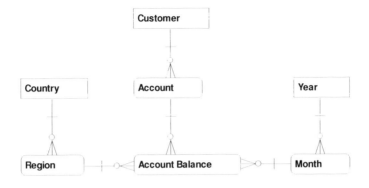

Figure 8.4 Financial dimensional CDM using the same notation as the relational CDM

Concept definitions:

Account Balance	An account balance is a financial record of how much money a customer has with our bank at the end of a given time period such as someone's checking account balance at the end of a month.
Country	A country is a recognized nation with its own government, occupying a particular territory, which is included in the ISO country code listing.
Region	A region is our bank's own definition of dividing a country into smaller pieces for branch assignment or reporting purposes.
Customer	A customer is a person or organization who obtains our product for resale. A person or organization must have obtained at least one product from us to be considered a customer. That is, prospects are not customers. Also, once a customer, always a customer, so even customers that have not obtained anything in 50 years are still considered customers. The customer is different than the consumer, who purchases the product for consumption as opposed to resale.
Account	An account is a contractual arrangement by which our bank holds funds on behalf of a customer.
Year	A year is a period of time containing 365 days, consistent with the Gregorian calendar.
Month	A month is each of the twelve named periods into which a year is divided.

The model in Figure 8.4 was created using the same symbols we used for the relational, which is called Information Engineering (IE) notation. Some data modeling tools such as ER/Studio contain a separate set of symbols we can use to build the dimensional model as shown in Figure 8.5.

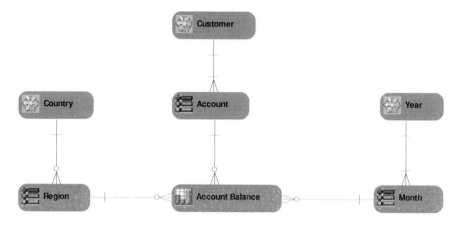

Figure 8.5 Financial dimensional CDM using dimensional notation

The relationship lines have the same appearance as in Figure 8.4, yet the entities appear as bub-tangles. There are several different types of entities on a dimensional model, each type distinguished with a different icon.

Account Balance is an example of a fact table (on a conceptual and logical data model often called a "meter"). The icon for a meter in ER/Studio is the graph symbol because we are measuring the health of a business process. A meter is an entity containing a related set of measures. It is not a person, place, event, or thing, as we find on the relational model. Instead, it is a bucket of common measures. As a group, common measures address a business process such as Profitability, Employee Satisfaction, or Sales. The meter is so important to the dimensional model that the name of the meter is often the name of the application: the **Sales** meter, the Sales Data Mart.

Region, **Account**, and **Month** are examples of dimensions, distinguished by the three horizontal lines icon. A dimension is a subject whose purpose is to add meaning to the measures. All of the different ways of filtering, sorting, and summing measures make use of dimensions.

Country, **Customer**, and **Year** are examples of snowflakes, distinguished by the snowflake icon. These are higher levels in a hierarchy. A hierarchy is when a higher level can contain many lower levels but a lower level can belong to, at most, one higher level. These higher levels indicate that we can view the measures in the meter at these levels as well. For example, we can view **Account Balance Amount** at the **Country**, **Customer**, and **Year** level.

We will explain additional dimensional terminology in Chapter 9, Logical Data Models. When I build a dimensional data model, I use the notation I think my audience will best understand. I will use the IE notation when my audience is already very familiar with this modeling notation from the relational data models but often use the dimensional data modeling notation when my audience is less familiar with data modeling.

CREATING A CONCEPTUAL DATA MODEL

There are five steps to conceptual data modeling as illustrated in Figure 8.6.

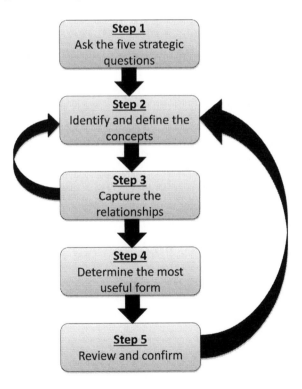

Figure 8.6 Five steps to conceptual data modeling

Before you begin any project, there are five strategic questions that must be asked (Step 1). These questions are a prerequisite to the success of any application effort. Next, identify all of the concepts within the scope of the application you are building (Step 2). Make sure each concept is clearly and completely defined. Then determine how these concepts are related to each other (Step 3). Often, you will need to go back to Step 2 at this point because in capturing relationships you often come up with new concepts—and then there are new relationships between these new concepts. Next, decide the most useful form for making sure your work during this phase is put to good use (Step 4). Someone will need to review your work and use your findings during development, so deciding on the most useful form is an important step. As a final step, review your work to get approval to move on to the logical data modeling phase (Step 5).

STEP 1: ASK THE FIVE STRATEGIC QUESTIONS

There are five questions that need to be asked (refer to the example in Figure 8.7):

1. **What is the application going to do?** Precisely and clearly document the answer to this question in a few sentences. Make sure to include whether you are replacing an existing system, delivering new functionality, integrating several existing applications together, etc. Always "begin with the end in mind," and so you know exactly what you are going to deliver. This question helps determine the scope of the application.

2. **"As is" or "to be"?** You need to know if there is a requirement to understand and model the current business environment (that is, the "as is" view) or to understand and model a proposed business environment (that is, the "to be" view).

3. **Is analytics a requirement?** Analytics, in informal terms, is the field of playing with numbers. That is, taking measurements such as **Gross Sales Amount** or **Inventory Count** and viewing them at different levels of granularity such as by day or year. If there is a requirement for analytics, at least part of your solution needs to be dimensional. Relational modeling focuses on business rules, and dimensional modeling focuses on business questions.

4. **Who is the audience?** That is, who is the person or group who is the validator and can confirm your understanding of the CDM, and who will be the users of the CDM? It is a good policy with anything you produce to determine early on who will check your work (the validators) and who will be the recipient or users of your work. This question will ensure you choose the ideal display format for your conceptual data model. Note that if the validators and users vary considerably in their technical expertise, you may need more than one form for the CDM.

5. **Flexibility or simplicity?** In terms of design, there is always a balancing act between flexibility and simplicity. If you are leaning more towards flexibility, you will most likely use some generic terms such as **Event** instead of **Order** or **Person** instead of **Employee**.

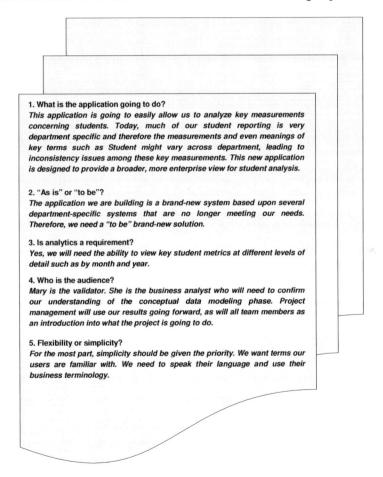

1. What is the application going to do?
This application is going to easily allow us to analyze key measurements concerning students. Today, much of our student reporting is very department specific and therefore the measurements and even meanings of key terms such as Student might vary across department, leading to inconsistency issues among these key measurements. This new application is designed to provide a broader, more enterprise view for student analysis.

2. "As is" or "to be"?
The application we are building is a brand-new system based upon several department-specific systems that are no longer meeting our needs. Therefore, we need a "to be" brand-new solution.

3. Is analytics a requirement?
Yes, we will need the ability to view key student metrics at different levels of detail such as by month and year.

4. Who is the audience?
Mary is the validator. She is the business analyst who will need to confirm our understanding of the conceptual data modeling phase. Project management will use our results going forward, as will all team members as an introduction into what the project is going to do.

5. Flexibility or simplicity?
For the most part, simplicity should be given the priority. We want terms our users are familiar with. We need to speak their language and use their business terminology.

Figure 8.7 Sample answers to the five strategic questions for a student application

STEP 2: IDENTIFY AND DEFINE THE CONCEPTS

Now that we have direction, we can work with the business experts to identify the concepts within the scope of the application and come up with an agreed-upon definition for each concept.

For Relational

To identify and define the relational concepts, recall our definition of an entity as a noun or noun phrase that fits into one of six categories: who, what, when, where, why, or how. We can use these six categories to create a Concept Template for capturing the entities on our conceptual data model. See Table 8.2.

Who?	What?	When?	Where?	Why?	How?
1.	1.	1.	1.	1.	1.
2.	2.	2.	2.	2.	2.
3.	3.	3.	3.	3.	3.
4.	4.	4.	4.	4.	4.
5.	5.	5.	5.	5.	5.

Table 8.2 Concept template

Table 8.3 contains a completed concept template for an Account System.

Account Project Concepts

Who?	What?	When?	Where?	Why?	How?
1. Customer	1. Account	1. Account Open Date	1. Branch	1. Check Debit	1. Check
2.	2.	2.	2.	2. Deposit Credit	2. Deposit Slip
3.	3.	3.	3.	3. Interest Credit	3. Withdrawal Slip
4.	4.	4.	4.	4. Monthly Statement Fee	4. Bank Account Statement
5.	5.	5.	5.	5. Withdrawal Debit	5. Account Balance

Table 8.3 Completed concept template for an account application

Here are some of the concept definitions:

Account	An account is an arrangement by which our bank holds funds on behalf of a customer. This arrangement includes the amount of funds we hold on behalf of a customer as well as a historical perspective of all of the transactions that have impacted this amount such as deposits and withdrawals. An account is structured for a particular purpose such as for stock investing, which is called a "brokerage account"; for interest-bearing, which is called a "savings account"; and for check writing, which is called a "checking account." An account can only be one of these types. That is, an account cannot be both checking and savings.
Account Balance	An account balance is a financial record of how much money a customer has with our bank at the end of a given time period such as someone's checking account balance at the end of a month. The account balance is impacted by many types of transactions including deposits and withdrawals. The account balance amount is restricted to just a single account. That is, if we wanted to know Bob the customer's net worth to our bank, we would need to sum the account balances for all of Bob's accounts.
Account Open Date	The day, month, and year that a customer first opens their account. This is the date that appears on the new account application form and is often not the same date as when the account first becomes active and useable. It may take 24-48 hours after the application is submitted for the account to be useable. The account open date can be any day of the week including a date when the bank is closed (if the customer submits the application using our website off hours).
Bank Account Statement	A periodic record of the events that have impacted the account. Events include withdrawals, deposits, etc. The bank account statement is usually issued monthly and includes the beginning account balance, a record of all events, and the ending account balance. Also listed are bank fees and, if applicable, any interest accrued.

For Dimensional

For dimensional, we need to determine the specific business questions that must be answered. For example, imagine that we work with the business analysts for a university and identify the following four questions:

1. Show me the number of students receiving financial aid by department and semester for the last five years. [From Financial Aid Office]

2. Show me the number of students on full or partial scholarship by department and semester for the last four years. [From Accounting Department]

3. How many students graduated by department and semester over the last three years? [From Alumni Affairs]

4. How many students applied to the university over the last ten years? I want to compare applications from high school students vs. other universities. [From Admissions Department]

STEP 3: CAPTURE THE RELATIONSHIPS

For Relational

Relational is all about capturing the business rules, so our objective at the relational conceptual level is to determine which entities relate to each other and then articulate the rules. For each relationship line on our model, we find ourselves asking up to eight questions: two on participation, two on optionality, and up to four questions on subtyping. See Table 8.4.

Question	Yes	No
Can an Entity A be related to more than one Entity B?		
Can an Entity B be related to more than one Entity A?		
Can an Entity A exist without an Entity B?		
Can an Entity B exist without an Entity A?		
Are there examples of Entity A that would be valuable to show?		
Are there examples of Entity B that would be valuable to show?		
Does an Entity A go through a lifecycle?		
Does an Entity B go through a lifecycle?		

Table 8.4 Eight questions to ask for each conceptual relationship

The first two questions are on participation, and the answers to these questions will determine whether there is a one or many symbol on the relationship line next to each entity. For example, if "Yes" Entity A can be related to more than one Entity B then there will be a many symbol on the relationship line next to Entity B.

The next two questions are on optionality, and the answers to these questions will determine whether there is a zero symbol on the relationship line next to either entity. For example, if "Yes" Entity A can exist without Entity B, then there will be a zero symbol on the relationship line next to Entity B.

The answers to the next four questions will determine where we introduce subtyping on the conceptual data model. When examples will aid communication or if it is important to explain the lifecycle of a concept, then subtyping needs to be added to the model.

Table 8.5 shows an example for our Account application.

Question	Yes	No
Can a Customer own more than one Account?	✓	
Can an Account be owned by more than one Customer?	✓	
Can a Customer exist without an Account?	✓	
Can an Account exist without a Customer?		✓
Are there examples of Customer that would be valuable to show?		✓
Are there examples of Account that would be valuable to show?	✓	
Does a Customer go through a lifecycle?	✓	
Does an Account go through a lifecycle?		✓
Can a Branch contain more than one Account?	✓	
Can an Account belong to more than one Branch?		✓
Can a Branch exist without an Account?	✓	
Can an Account exist without a Branch?		✓
Are there examples of Branch that would be valuable to show?		✓
Does a Branch go through a lifecycle?		✓

Table 8.5 Partial set of answers to the eight questions for an account application

Shading was used in the above table as a way to group the questions for each relationship together. That is, the unshaded rows answer the questions on the relationship between **Customer** and **Account** and the shaded rows answer the questions on the relationship between **Branch** and **Account**. Notice also since we answered the example and lifecycle questions for **Account** for

Account's relationship with **Customer**, we did not need to ask these questions again when **Account** is related with **Branch**.

For Dimensional

For dimensional, we need to take the business questions we identified in the prior step and then create a Grain Matrix. A grain matrix is a spreadsheet where the measures from the business questions become columns and the dimensional levels from the business questions become rows. The purpose of a grain matrix is to efficiently scope analytic applications. It is possible to elicit hundreds of business questions, and after plotting these questions on a grain matrix, we make the observation that questions from different departments can actually be very similar to each other. By consolidating questions, we can scope applications that address the needs for more than one department. Table 8.6 contains a completed grain matrix for our Student Application.

	Student Count
Financial Aid Indicator	1
Semester	1, 2, 3
Year	1, 2, 3, 4
Department	1, 2, 3
Scholarship Indicator	2
Graduation Indicator	3
High School Application Indicator	4
University Application Indicator	4

Table 8.6 Completed grain matrix for a student application

In this grain matrix, we took each of the four questions from Step 2 and parsed them so that the measure from each question (**Student Count**) became a column and the levels of detail in each question became rows. The numbers in the grain matrix refer back to the question numbers.

STEP 4: DETERMINE THE MOST USEFUL FORM

Someone will need to review your work and use your findings during development, so deciding the most useful form is an important step. We know the users for the model after getting an answer to Strategic Question #4 from

Step 1: *Who is our audience?* What person or group is the validator and can confirm our understanding of the CDM, and who will be the users of the CDM?

For Relational

If the validator and users are already familiar with data modeling notation, the decision is an easy one: use the traditional data modeling notation they are comfortable with such as this example in Figure 8.8. Refer back to the answers from Step 3 to see how these answers impacted the cardinality on this model. Subtyping has been introduced for **Account** because there was a need to show examples of **Account** and subtyping was introduced for **Customer** because **Customer** goes through a lifecycle.

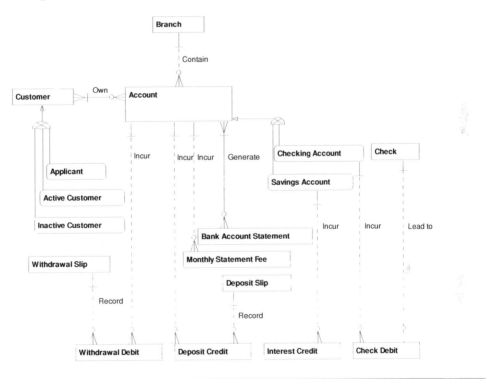

Figure 8.8 Traditional data modeling notation

However, very frequently at the conceptual level, the validator (and sometimes the users too) is not familiar with traditional data modeling notation or simply doesn't want to see a data model. In these situations, be creative with how you display the model, coming up with a visual that the audience for the model would understand. For example, Figure 8.9 contains a business sketch that can be used instead of the traditional data modeling notation.

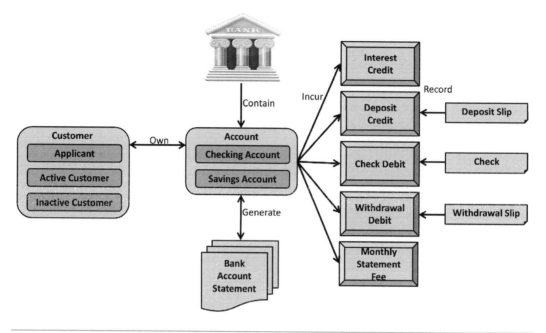

Figure 8.9 Business sketch instead of the traditional data model

Instead of the word "Branch" inside a rectangle, this model contains a picture of a branch. Instead of subtyping symbols, the subtypes are shown inside the supertype. Instead of the word "Bank Account Statement" inside a rectangle, a shape which represents a large document is used. Different shapes are used for smaller documents such as a **Withdrawal Slip** and button shapes are used to represent transactions such as an **Interest Credit**.

For Dimensional

Figure 8.10 shows the dimensional model with the traditional notation and Figure 8.11 shows my favorite conceptual dimensional form, the Axis Technique.

The Axis Technique is when you put the business process you are measuring in the center (e.g. **Student Attrition**) with each axis representing a dimension. The notches on each axis represent the levels of detail that are required to see the measures in the meter. This form works very well when the audience has limited exposure to data modeling.

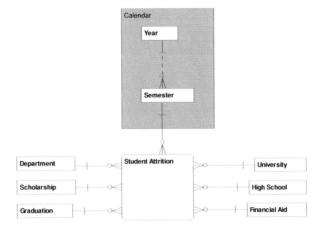

Figure 8.10 Traditional data modeling notation

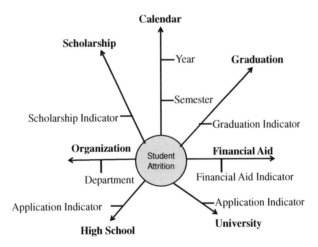

Figure 8.11 Axis Technique

STEP 5: REVIEW AND CONFIRM

The validators will need to review our data model and frequently during this step there are changes that require us to go back to Step 2 and refine the concepts. Most likely (and hopefully) the validators were involved during the process of building the conceptual, and therefore in many cases this review step becomes a formality.

EXERCISE 8: BUILDING A CDM

Identify an area within your organization that is in desperate need of a CDM and build it for them using the five-step approach from this chapter.

Key Points

- ✓ A concept is a key term that is both basic and critical to your audience.

- ✓ A conceptual data model (CDM) is a set of symbols and text that represents key concepts and the rules binding these key concepts for a specific business or application scope and for a particular audience.

- ✓ The relational CDM includes concepts, their definitions, and the relationships that capture the rules binding these concepts. The dimensional CDM includes concepts, their definitions, and the navigation paths required to analyze measures at different levels of detail.

- ✓ Follow the five-step approach to building a CDM.

What does business need?
Forget the technology
Enter logical

The highlighted row in Table 9.1 shows the focus of this chapter, which is the logical data model (LDM).

	Relational	Dimensional
Conceptual Data Model (CDM)	'One-pager' on business rules	'One-pager' on navigation
Logical Data Model (LDM)	**Detailed business solution on business rules**	**Detailed business solution on navigation**
Physical Data Model (PDM)	Detailed technical solution	

Table 9.1 The Logical Data Model is the focus of this chapter

A LDM takes the business need defined on a conceptual data model down to the next level of a business solution. That is, once you understand at a broad level the scope of an effort and what business people require to solve their problem, the next step is to come up with a solution for them in the form of a LDM. The logical data model is explained, along with a comparison of relational and dimensional mindsets. Then, for relational models, the techniques of normalization and abstraction are discussed. I conclude by answering Frequently Asked Questions (FAQ) on dimensional modeling, which leads to explaining terms such as conformed dimensions and factless facts.

LOGICAL DATA MODEL EXPLAINED

A logical data model (LDM) is a business solution to a business problem. It is how the modeler captures the business requirements without complicating the model with implementation concerns such as software and hardware.

On the conceptual data model, we might learn, for example, what the terms, business rules, and scope would be for a new order entry system. After understanding the requirements for the order entry system, we create a LDM containing all of the attributes and business rules needed to deliver the application. For example, the conceptual data model will show that a **Customer** may place one or many **Orders**. The LDM will capture all of the details behind **Customer** and **Order** such as the customer's name, their address, the order number, and what is being ordered.

While building the LDM, questions or issues may arise having to do with specific hardware or software such as:

- We have a big data scenario, so how can we process a lot of data very quickly and then afterwards analyze it very quickly?
- How can we make this information secure?
- How can we answer this business question in less than two seconds?

These questions focus on hardware and software. Although they need to be documented, they are not addressed until we are ready to start the physical data model. The reason these questions depend on technology is because if hardware and software were infinitely efficient and secure, these questions would never be raised.

RELATIONAL AND DIMENSIONAL LOGICAL DATA MODELS

Recall from this section's introduction that relational data modeling is the process of capturing how the business *works* by precisely representing business rules, while dimensional data modeling is the process of capturing how the business is *monitored* by precisely representing navigation. There are both relational and dimensional logical data models.

You have seen examples of both relational and dimensional conceptual data models (recall Figures 8.3 and 8.4 from the chapter on conceptual data modeling); Figures 9.1 and 9.2 show these two examples at a logical level. Let's go through how each of these are built, starting with relational.

RELATIONAL LDM EXAMPLE

The relational logical data model includes entities along with their definitions, relationships, and attributes. For example, Figure 9.1 contains part of a financial relational LDM.

Business Rules (listed in the order we would typically walk someone through the model):

- Each **Customer** may own one or many **Accounts**.
- Each **Account** must be owned by one or many **Customers**.
- Each **Account** may contain one or many **Account Balances**.
- Each **Account Balance** must belong to one **Account**.

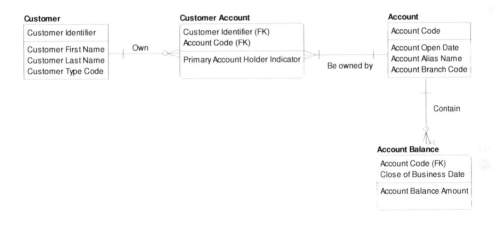

Figure 9.1 Financial relational LDM subset

DIMENSIONAL LDM EXAMPLE

Figure 9.2 shows a dimensional LDM.

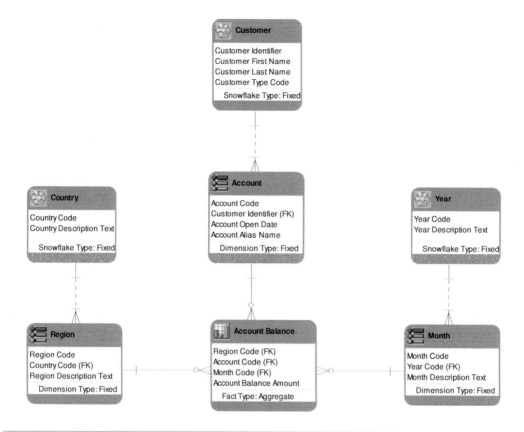

Figure 9.2 Financial dimensional LDM

We take measures such as **Account Balance Amount** up and down hierarchies. In this case, we'd like to see **Account Balance Amount** at a **Region**, **Account**, and **Month** level and then have the ability to navigate to higher levels such as viewing **Account Balance Amount** at a **Country** level instead of the more granular **Region** level.

Region is an interesting level to discuss. Often when building a dimensional data model, we trace back the measures and ways of looking at these measures to a relational data model that will eventually be the source for the dimensional data. On our relational data model in Figure 9.1, we have an **Account Branch Code** in the **Account** entity. On the corresponding dimensional data model, however, there is no need to know what the branch code is—only the higher level of **Region**. Therefore, each **Region** has to be derived from the corresponding **Branch Code** because in this case, **Region** was requested as an easier level to navigate than **Branch**.

CREATING A RELATIONAL LOGICAL DATA MODEL

The two techniques used to build the relational logical data model are normalization and abstraction.

NORMALIZATION

When I turned 12, I received a trunk full of baseball cards as a birthday present from my parents. I was delighted, not just because there may have been a Hank Aaron or Pete Rose buried somewhere in that trunk, but because I loved to organize the cards. I categorized each card according to year and team. Organizing the cards in this way gave me a deep understanding of the players and their teams. To this day, I can answer many baseball card trivia questions.

Normalization, in general, is the process of applying a set of rules with the goal of organizing *something*. I was normalizing the baseball cards according to year and team. We can also apply a set of rules and normalize the attributes within our organizations. Just as those baseball cards lay unsorted in that trunk, our companies have huge numbers of attributes spread throughout departments and applications. The rules applied to normalizing the baseball cards entailed first sorting by year and then by team within a year. The rules for normalizing our attributes can be boiled down to a single sentence:

Make sure every attribute is <u>single-valued</u> and <u>provides a fact completely</u> and <u>only</u> about its primary key.

The underlined terms require more of an explanation.

<u>Single-valued</u> means an attribute must contain only one piece of information. If **Consumer Name** contains both the consumer's first and last name, for example, we must split **Consumer Name** into two attributes: **Consumer First Name** and **Consumer Last Name**.

<u>Provides a fact</u> means that a given primary key value will always return no more than one of every attribute that is identified by this key. If a **Customer Identifier** value of `123` for example, returns three customer last names (`Smith`, `Jones`, and `Roberts`), it violates this part of the normalization definition.

<u>Completely</u> means that the minimal set of attributes that uniquely identify an instance of the entity is present in the primary key. If, for example, there are two attributes in an entity's primary key, but only one is needed for uniqueness, the attribute that is not needed for uniqueness should be removed from the primary key.

<u>Only</u> means that each attribute must provide a fact about the primary key and nothing else. That is, there can be no hidden dependencies. For example, assume an **Order** is identified by an **Order Number**. Within **Order**, there are many attributes including **Order Scheduled Delivery Date**, **Order Actual Delivery Date**, and **Order On Time Indicator**. **Order On Time Indicator** contains either a `Yes` or a `No`, providing a fact about whether the **Order Actual Delivery Date** is less than or equal to the **Order Scheduled Delivery Date**. **Order On Time Indicator**, therefore, provides a fact about **Order Actual Delivery Date** and **Order Scheduled Delivery Date**, not directly about **Order Number**. **Order On Time Indicator** is an example of a derived attribute, meaning it is calculated. Derived attributes are removed from a normalized model.

So a general definition for normalization is that it is a series of rules for organizing something. As mentioned, the series of rules can be summarized as: *Every attribute is single-valued and provides a fact completely and only about its primary key.* An informal definition I frequently use for normalizing is "A formal process of asking business questions." We cannot determine if every attribute is single-valued and provides a fact completely and only about its primary key unless we understand the data. To understand the data, we usually need to ask lots of questions. Even for an apparently simple attribute such as **Phone Number,** for example, we can ask many questions:

- Whose phone number is this?
- Do you always have to have a phone number?

- Can you have more than one phone number?
- Do you ever recognize the area code as separate from the rest of the phone number?
- Do you ever need to see phone numbers outside a given country?
- What type of phone number is this? That is, is it a fax number, mobile number, etc.?
- Does the time of day matter? For example, do we need to distinguish between the phone numbers to use during working hours and outside working hours? Of course, that would lead to a discussion on what we mean by "working hours."

To ensure that every attribute is single-valued and provides a fact completely and only about its primary key, we apply a series of rules in small steps, where each step (or level of normalization) checks something that moves us towards our goal. Most data professionals would agree that the full set of normalization levels is the following:

> first normal form (1NF)
> second normal form (2NF)
> third normal form (3NF)
> Boyce/Codd normal form (BCNF)
> fourth normal form (4NF)
> fifth normal form (5NF)

Each level of normalization includes the lower levels of rules that precede it. If a model is in 5NF, it is also in 4NF, BCNF, and so on. Even though there are higher levels of normalization than 3NF, many interpret the term *normalized* to mean 3NF. This is because the higher levels of normalization (that is, BCNF, 4NF, and 5NF) cover specific situations that occur much less frequently than the first three levels. Therefore, to keep things simple, this chapter focuses only on first through third normal forms.

Initial Chaos

I would describe the trunk of baseball cards I received as being in a chaotic state because there was no order to the cards. Just a bunch of cards thrown in a large box. I removed the chaos by organizing the cards. The term *chaos* can be applied to any unorganized pile, including attributes. We may have a strong understanding of each of the attributes, such as their name and definition, but we lack knowledge as to which entity the attribute should be assigned. When I pick out a 1978 Pete Rose from the box and put this card in the 1978 pile, I start bringing order were there was chaos—similar to assigning **Customer Last Name** to the customer pile (called the **Customer** entity).

Let's walk through an example. Figure 9.3 contains a bunch of what appears to be employee attributes.

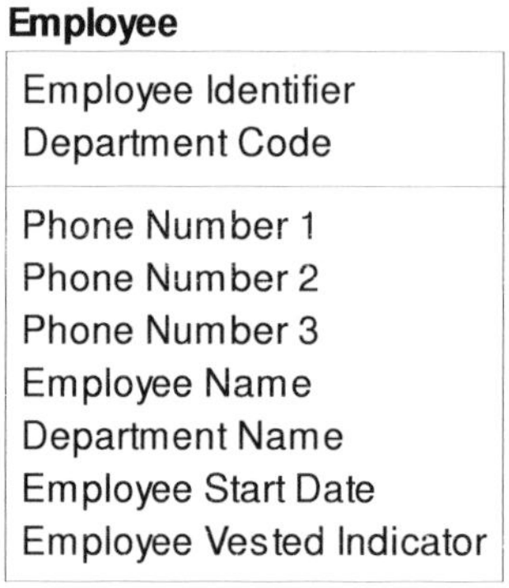

Employee

Employee Identifier
Department Code

Phone Number 1
Phone Number 2
Phone Number 3
Employee Name
Department Name
Employee Start Date
Employee Vested Indicator

Figure 9.3 Initial chaotic state

Often definitions are of poor quality or missing completely, and let's assume that this is the case with this **Employee** entity. We are told, however, that **Employee Vested Indicator** captures whether an **Employee** is eligible for retirement benefits (a value of Y for "yes" means the employee is eligible, and a value of N for "no" means the employee is not eligible) and this indicator is derived from the employee's start date. For example, if an employee has worked for the company for at least five years then this indicator contains the value Y.

What is lacking at this point, and what will be solved though normalization, is putting these attributes into the right entities.

It is very helpful to have some sample values for each of these attributes, so let's assume the spreadsheet in Table 9.2 is a representative set of employee values.

Emp Id	Dept Cd	Phone 1	Phone 2	Phone 3	Emp Name	Dept Name	Emp Start Date	Emp Vested Ind
123	A	973-555-1212	678-333-3333	343-222-1111	Henry Winkler	Data Admin	4/1/2012	N
789	A	732-555-3333	678-333-3333	343-222-1111	Steve Martin	Data Admin	3/5/2007	Y
565	B	333-444-1111	516-555-1212	343-222-1111	Mary Smith	Data Warehouse	2/25/2006	Y
744	A	232-222-2222	678-333-3333	343-222-1111	Bob Jones	Data Admin	5/5/2011	N

Table 9.2 Sample employees

First Normal Form (1NF)

Recall that the series of rules can be summarized as: *Every attribute is single-valued and provides a fact completely and only about its primary key*. First Normal Form (1NF) is the "single-valued" part. It means that for a given primary-key value, we can find, at most, one of every attribute that depends on that primary key.

Ensuring each attribute provides a fact about its primary key includes correcting the more blatant issue shown in Table 9.2 as well as addressing repeating groups and multi-valued attributes. Specifically, the modeler needs to:

- **Move repeating attributes to a new entity**. When there are two or more of the same attribute in the same entity, they are called repeating attributes. The reason repeating attributes violate 1NF is that for a given primary key value, we are getting more than one value back for the same attribute. Repeating attributes often take a sequence number as part of their name such as phone number in this employee example. We can find ourselves asking many questions just to determine if there are any repeating attributes we need to address. We can have a question template like this: "Can a [[insert entity name here]] have more than one [[insert attribute name here]]?" So these are all valid questions in our employee example:

    o Can an **Employee** have more than one **Employee Identifier**?
    o Can an **Employee** have more than one **Department Code**?

- ○ Can an **Employee** have more than one **Phone Number**?
- ○ Can an **Employee** have more than one **Employee Name**?
- ○ Can an **Employee** have more than one **Department Name**?
- ○ Can an **Employee** have more than one **Employee Start Date**?
- ○ Can an **Employee** have more than one **Employee Vested Indicator**?

- **Separate multi-valued attributes**. *Multi-valued* means that within the same attribute we are storing at least two distinct values. In other words, there are at least two different business concepts hiding in one attribute. For example, **Employee Name** may contain both a first name and last name. **Employee First Name** and **Employee Last Name** can be considered distinct attributes; and therefore, Henry Winkler is multi-valued because it contains both Henry and Winkler. We may find ourselves asking many questions just to determine if there are any multi-valued attributes we need to identify. We can use another question template: "Does a [[insert attribute name here]] contain more than one piece of business information?" So these are all valid questions in our employee example:

  - ○ Does an **Employee Identifier** contain more than one piece of business information?
  - ○ Does a **Department Code** contain more than one piece of business information?
  - ○ Does a **Phone Number** contain more than one piece of business information?
  - ○ Does an **Employee Name** contain more than one piece of business information?
  - ○ Does a **Department Name** contain more than one piece of business information?
  - ○ Does an **Employee Start Date** contain more than one piece of business information?
  - ○ Does an **Employee Vested Indicator** contain more than one piece of business information?

After talking with a business expert and answering these questions based on the sample data from Table 9.2, we update the model which appears in Figure 9.4.

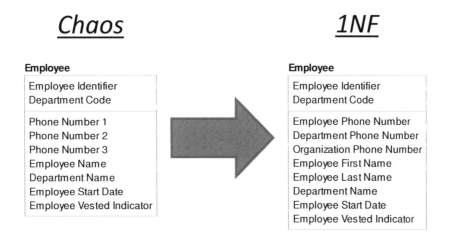

Figure 9.4 From Chaos to 1NF

We learned that although **Phone Number 1**, **Phone Number 2**, and **Phone Number 3** appear as repeating attributes, they are really three different pieces of information based upon the sample values we were given. **Phone Number 3** contained the same value for all four employees, and we learned after validating with the business expert that this is the organization's phone number. **Phone Number 2** varied by department, so this attribute was renamed to **Department Phone Number**. **Phone Number 3** is different for each employee, and we learned that this is the **Employee Phone Number**. We also were told that **Employee Name** does contain more than one piece of information and therefore should be split into **Employee First Name** and **Employee Last Name**.

Second Normal Form (2NF)

Recall that the series of rules can be summarized as: *Every attribute is single-valued and provides a fact completely and only about its primary key*. First Normal Form (1NF) is the "single-valued" part. Second Normal Form (2NF) is the "completely" part. This means each entity must have the minimal set of attributes that uniquely identifies each entity instance.

As with 1NF, we will find ourselves asking many questions to determine if we have the minimal primary key. We can use another question template: "Are all of the attributes in the primary key needed to retrieve a single instance of [[insert attribute name here]]?" In the Employee example shown in Figure 9.4, the "minimal set of primary key instances" are **Employee Identifier** and **Department Code.**

So these are all valid questions for our employee example:

- Are both **Employee Identifier** and **Department Code** needed to retrieve a single instance of **Employee Phone Number**?
- Are both **Employee Identifier** and **Department Code** needed to retrieve a single instance of **Department Phone Number**?
- Are both **Employee Identifier** and **Department Code** needed to retrieve a single instance of **Organization Phone Number**?
- Are both **Employee Identifier** and **Department Code** needed to retrieve a single instance of **Employee First Name**?
- Are both **Employee Identifier** and **Department Code** needed to retrieve a single instance of **Employee Last Name**?
- Are both **Employee Identifier** and **Department Code** needed to retrieve a single instance of **Department Name**?
- Are both **Employee Identifier** and **Department Code** needed to retrieve a single instance of **Employee Start Date**?
- Are both **Employee Identifier** and **Department Code** needed to retrieve a single instance of **Employee Vested Indicator**?

Normalization is a process of asking business questions. In this example, we could not complete 2NF without asking the business "Can an **Employee** work for more than one **Department** at the same time?" If the answer is "Yes" or "Sometimes," then the first model in Figure 9.5 on the left is accurate. If the answer is "No," then the second model prevails.

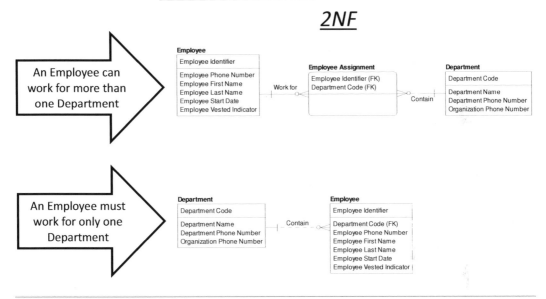

Figure 9.5 Employee example in 2NF

Third Normal Form (3NF)

Recall that the series of rules can be summarized as: *Every attribute is single-valued and provides a fact completely and only about its primary key.* First Normal Form (1NF) is the "single-valued" part. Second Normal Form (2NF) is the "completely" part. Third Normal Form (3NF) is the "only" part.

3NF requires the removal of hidden dependencies. Each attribute must be directly dependent on the primary key and not directly dependent on any other attributes within the same entity.

The data model is a communication tool. The relational logical data model communicates which attributes are facts about the primary key and only the primary key. Hidden dependencies complicate the model and make it difficult to determine how to retrieve values for each attribute.

To resolve a hidden dependency, you will either need to remove the attribute that is a fact about the non-primary key attribute(s) from the model or you will need to create a new entity with a different primary key for the attribute that is dependent on the non-primary key attribute(s).

As with 1NF and 2NF, we will find ourselves asking many questions to uncover hidden dependencies. We can use another question template: "Is [[insert attribute name here]] a fact about any other attribute in this same entity?"

So these are all valid questions for our contact example:

- Is **Employee Phone Number** a fact about any other attribute in **Employee**?
- Is **Organization Phone Number** a fact about any other attribute in **Department**?
- Is **Department Phone Number** a fact about any other attribute in **Department**?
- Is **Employee First Name** a fact about any other attribute in **Employee**?
- Is **Employee Last Name** a fact about any other attribute in **Employee**?
- Is **Department Name** a fact about any other attribute in **Department**?
- Is **Employee Start Date** a fact about any other attribute in **Employee**?
- Is **Employee Vested Indicator** a fact about any other attribute in **Employee**?

Note that **Employee Vested Indicator** may be a fact about **Employee Start Date** as **Employee Vested Indicator** can be calculated Y or N based upon the employee's start date. Figure 9.6 shows the model now in 3NF after removing the derived attribute, **Employee Vested Indicator.**

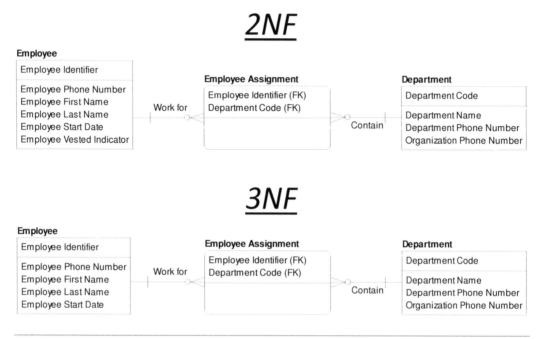

Figure 9.6 Employee example in 3NF

You will find that the more you normalize, the more you go from applying rules sequentially to applying them in parallel. For example, instead of first applying 1NF to your model everywhere, then when you are done applying 2NF, and so on, you will find yourself looking to apply all levels at once. This can be done by looking at each entity and making sure the primary key is correct and contains a minimal set of attributes and that all attributes are facts about only the primary key.

ABSTRACTION

Normalization is a mandatory technique on the relational logical data model. Abstraction is an optional technique. Abstraction brings flexibility to your data models by redefining and combining some of the attributes, entities, and relationships within the model into more generic terms.

For example, we can take our normalized data model and abstract **Employee** into **Party** and **Role**, as shown in Figure 9.7.

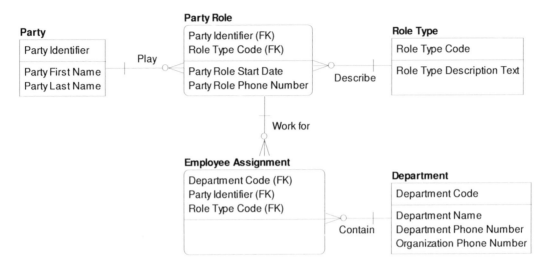

Figure 9.7 Employee abstracted

Notice the extra flexibility we gain with abstraction. By abstracting **Employee** into the **Party Role** concept, we can accommodate additional roles without changes to our model and most likely without changes to our application. Roles such as **Contractor** and **Consumer** can be added gracefully without updates to our model. However, this extra flexibility does come with a price. Actually, three high prices:

- **Loss of communication**. The concepts we abstract are no longer represented explicitly on the model. That is, when we abstract, we often convert column names to entity instances. For example, **Employee** is no longer an explicit entity but is instead an entity instance of **Party Role**, with a **Role Type Code** value of 03 for Employee. One of the main reasons we model is to aid communication, but abstracting can definitely hinder communication.

- **Loss of business rules**. When we abstract, we can also lose business rules. To be more specific, the rules we enforced on the data model before abstraction now need to be enforced through other means such as through programming code. If we wanted to enforce that an **Employee** must have a **Start Date,** for example, we can no longer enforce this rule through the abstracted data model in Figure 9.7.

- **Additional development complexity.** Abstracting requires sophisticated development techniques to turn attributes into values when loading an abstract structure, or to turn values back into attributes when populating a structure from an abstract source. Imagine the work to populate **Party Role** from the source **Employee**. It would be much easier for a developer to load data from an entity called **Employee** into an entity called **Employee**. The code would be simpler and it would be very fast to load.

So although abstraction provides flexibility to an application, it does come with a cost. It makes the most sense to use abstraction when the modeler or analyst anticipates additional *types* of something coming in the near future. In the example from Figure 9.7, additional types of people might include **Contractor** and **Consumer**.

CREATING A DIMENSIONAL LOGICAL DATA MODEL

Recall the dimensional data model from earlier in this chapter, repeated here in Figure 9.8.

Account Balance is an example of a meter, which is an entity containing a related set of measures. It is not a person, place, event, or thing, as we find on the relational model. Instead, it is a bucket of common measures; in this case, just the measure **Account Balance Amount**. As a group, common measures address a business process such as **Profitability**, **Employee Satisfaction**, or **Sales**.

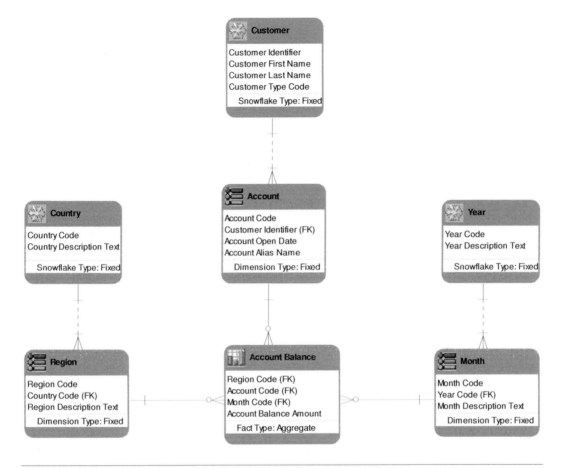

Figure 9.8 Financial dimensional LDM

A meter can be further classified into one these four types:

- **Aggregate**. Also known as a summarization, an aggregate contains information that is stored at a higher level of granularity than translation level details. Aggregates provide quick access to data and can be very user-friendly structures for users and reporting tools. **Account Balance** is an aggregate.

- **Atomic**. Contains the lowest level of detail available in the business, often the same level of detail that exists in operational systems such as order entry systems. An example of an atomic fact in the account balance subject area would be the individual bank account withdrawal and deposit transactions.

- **Cumulative**. Also known as accumulating, cumulative captures how long it takes to complete a business process. For example, tracking how long it takes from application through completion of a home mortgage application would be represented in a cumulative fact.

- **Snapshot**. Contains time-related information that details specific steps in the life of the entity. For example, snapshot information for a sale could contain information such as when the order was created, confirmed, shipped, delivered, and paid for.

Region, **Account**, and **Month** are examples of dimensions, distinguished by the three horizontal lines icon. A dimension is a subject whose purpose is to add meaning to the measures. All of the different ways of filtering, sorting, and summing measures make use of dimensions. Dimensions have their own attributes. A dimension can be further classified into one these six types:

- **Fixed Dimension**. Also known as a Type 0 Slowly Changing Dimension (SCD for short), a fixed dimension contains values that do not change over time. For example, **Gender** is a fixed dimension containing the values `Male` and `Female`.

- **Degenerate**. A dimension whose attribute(s) have been moved to the meter. A degenerate dimension is most common when the original dimension contained only a single data attribute such as a transaction identifier like an **Order Number**.

- **Multi-Valued**. A multi-valued dimension can help you model a situation where there are multiple values for an attribute or column. For example, a health care bill can have a line item of **Diagnosis** for which there could be multiple values. Best practice modeling dictates that there should be a single value for each line item. To model this multi-valued situation, you could create a multi-valued structure that captures the diagnosis information and weighs each diagnosis so that the total adds up to one.

- **Ragged**. In a ragged dimension, the parent of at least one member is missing from the level immediately above the member. Ragged dimensions allow for hierarchies of indeterminate depth such as organizational charts and parts explosions.

- **Shrunken**. A shrunken table is a version of the meter often containing attributes that are not measures. It is often used when there are large text strings that are at the same level of detail as the meter and are stored in a separate structure for space or query efficiency reasons.

- **Slowly Changing Type 0 through 6**. Slowly Changing Dimension (SCD) Type 0 is equivalent to the fixed dimension concept where values do not change over time. SCD Type 1 means we are only storing the current view and ignoring history. SCD Type 2 means we want all history (Type 2 is the Time Machine). SCD Type 3 means we want only some history such as the most current state and the previous state or the most current state and the original state. SCD Type 6 is when we have a complex dimension with varying history needs; for example, if part of the dimension is a Type 1, part is a Type 2, and part is a Type 3 (1 + 2 + 3 = 6). Types 0, 1, 2, and 3 are the building blocks for more advanced history requirements such as the Type 6.

Country, **Customer**, and **Year** are examples of snowflakes, distinguished by the snowflake icon. These are higher levels in a hierarchy. A hierarchy is when a higher level can contain many lower levels, but a lower level can belong to at most one higher level. These higher levels indicate that we can view the measures in the meter at these levels as well. For example, we can view **Account Balance Amount** at the **Country**, **Customer**, and **Year** level. Snowflakes can also have their own attributes.

EXERCISE 9: MODIFYING A LOGICAL DATA MODEL

You are working on a subset of a logical data model, as shown in Figure 9.9.

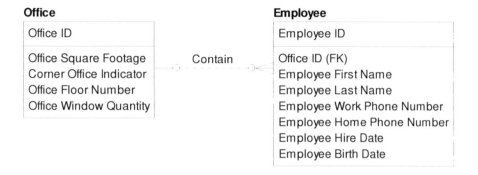

Figure 9.9 LDM subset

The relationship states:

- Each **Office** may contain one or many **Employees**.
- Each **Employee** may reside in one **Office**.

You need to add the attribute **Office First Occupied Date** to this model.

Here is the definition of **Office First Occupied Date:**

Office First Occupied Date *is the official date, as recorded in the Human Resources database, when a person first took up residence in an office. It must be a business day (that is, not a weekend day or holiday).*

The business expert in this area provides you with the following three rules that need to be captured on this model:

1. **Office First Occupied Date** is a mandatory field for each employee who has an office.
2. Only managers have an office and all managers have an office.
3. A manager has one and only one office.

Modify this model to accommodate this new attribute and these three business rules. When you are done, refer to the answers section at the back of the book.

Key Points

✓ A logical data model (LDM) represents a detailed business solution.

✓ A relational logical data model represents how the business works. A dimensional logical data model represents what the business is monitoring.

✓ Normalizing is a formal process of asking business questions. Normalization ensures that every attribute is a fact about the key (1NF), the whole key (2NF), and nothing but the key (3NF).

✓ Abstraction brings flexibility to your logical data models by redefining and combining some of the attributes, entities, and relationships within the model into more generic terms.

✓ There are a number of important terms unique to dimensional modeling including meters and dimensions.

✓ There are different types of meters including aggregate, atomic, cumulative, and snapshot.

✓ There are different types of dimensions including fixed dimension, degenerate, multi-valued, ragged, shrunken, and slow changing.

Let's get Physical
Compromise the Logical
Efficiency rules

The highlighted row in Table 10.1 shows the focus of this chapter, which is the physical data model (PDM).

	Relational	Dimensional
Conceptual Data Model (CDM)	"One-pager" on business rules	"One-pager" on navigation
Logical Data Model (LDM)	Detailed business solution on business rules	Detailed business solution on navigation
Physical Data Model (PDM)	**Detailed technical solution**	

Table 10.1 The Physical Data Model is the focus of this chapter

A PDM takes the business solution defined on a logical data model to the next level of a technical solution. That is, once you solve the problem independent of software and hardware concerns, you can then make adjustments for software and hardware.

This chapter will explain the most popular techniques for making adjustments to a business solution (LDM) to create an efficient technical solution (PDM). I will explain the PDM and then discuss the techniques of denormalization, views, indexing, and partitioning. Although these techniques apply to relational, dimensional, and NoSQL models, their names may differ depending on which type of model they are applied to. I will explain these terminology differences in this chapter as well.

PHYSICAL DATA MODEL EXPLAINED

The physical data model (PDM) is the logical data model compromised for specific software or hardware. On the CDM, we learn what the terms, business rules, and scope would be for a new order entry system. After understanding the need for an order entry system, we create a LDM representing the business solution. It contains all of the attributes and business rules needed to deliver the system. For example, the conceptual data model will show that a **Customer** may place one or many **Orders**. The LDM will capture all of the details behind **Customer** and **Order** such as the customer's name, their address, and the order number. After understanding the business solution, we move on to the technical solution and build the PDM. We may make some modifications to the **Customer** and **Order** structures, for example, for factors such as performance or storage.

While building the PDM, we address the issues that have to do with specific hardware or software such as:

- We have a big data scenario, so how can we process a lot of data very quickly and then afterwards analyze it very quickly?
- How can we make this information secure?
- How can we answer this business question in less than two seconds?

Note that in the early days of data modeling, when storage space was expensive and computers were slow, there were major modifications made to the PDM to make it work efficiently. In some cases, the PDM looked like it was for an entirely different application than the LDM. As technology improved, the PDM started looking more like the LDM. Faster and cheaper processors, cheaper and more generous disc space and system memory, and also specialized hardware have all played their part to make the physical look more like its logical counterpart. However, with big data processing and analytical tools becoming more mainstream, there is now (at least temporarily) a large difference again between physical and logical. Physical big data designs can even be file- or document-based to allow for fast loading and analyzing of data. So be aware of physical data models that are all in one table (or file); it may be the optimal design depending on the database technology.

RELATIONAL AND DIMENSIONAL PHYSICAL DATA MODELS

Recall from this section's introduction that relational data modeling is the process of capturing how the business *works* by precisely representing business rules, while dimensional data modeling is the process of capturing how the business is *monitored* by precisely representing navigation. There are both relational and dimensional physical data models.

You have seen examples of both relational and dimensional conceptual and logical data models (recall Figures 8.3 and 8.4 from the chapter on conceptual data modeling and Figures 9.1 and 9.2 from the chapter on logical data modeling). Figures 10.1 and 10.2 show these two examples at a physical level. Let's go through how each of these are built, starting with relational.

RELATIONAL PDM EXAMPLE

The relational PDM includes entities with their definitions, relationships, and columns along with their definitions. Note that in RDBMS the term *table* is used instead of the term *entity* and *column* instead of *attribute* on the physical data model. Figure 10.1 contains part of a financial relational PDM. Compromises such as combining **Customer** and **Account** into one structure were made to this model, most likely to improve data retrieval performance or to make it easier for developers to extract, transform, and load (ETL) data.

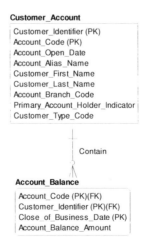

Figure 10.1 Financial relational PDM subset

DIMENSIONAL PDM EXAMPLE

To understand and document our reporting requirements, we can also build a dimensional PDM such as the example in Figure 10.2. This model, called a star schema (which we'll cover shortly), is similar to its logical counterpart except that each dimension from the dimensional LDM has been flattened on the model from Figure 9.2 into one structure.

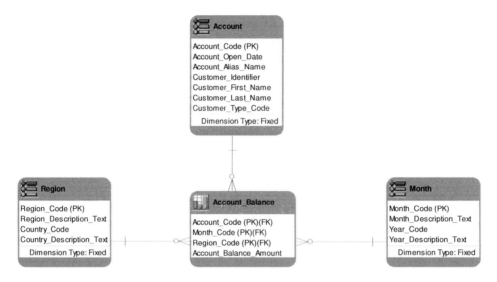

Figure 10.2 Financial dimensional PDM

DENORMALIZATION

Denormalization is the process of selectively violating normalization rules and reintroducing redundancy into the model (and, therefore, the database). This extra redundancy can reduce data retrieval time, which is the primary reason for denormalizing. We can also denormalize to create a more user-friendly model. For example, we might decide to denormalize company information into an entity containing employee information because usually when employee information is retrieved, company information is also retrieved. There are a number of different ways to denormalize. In this section, we'll discuss the two most common, Rolldown and Rollup.

Returning to our ice cream example, there is a small company that sells ice cream toppings. An **Offering** is an ice cream topping such as `chocolate sprinkles` or `hot fudge`. A **Category** is a way of organizing these toppings, such as the `Sprinkles` category containing the **Offerings** `Chocolate Sprinkles` and `Rainbow Sprinkles`. An **Offering** can belong to more than one **Category** as well, such as `Chocolate Sprinkles` belonging to both the `Sprinkles` and `Chocolate` **Categories**.

We will apply the rolldown and rollup techniques to **Offering**, **Category**, and **Assignment**. See Figure 10.3 for the normalized starting point and their physical counterparts using each of these two techniques. Note that **Category Priority Number** is the popularity rating of a **Category**, and **Assignment Priority Number** is the popularity of an **Offering** within a **Category**.

Our Normalized Starting Point:

Rolldown Denormalization:

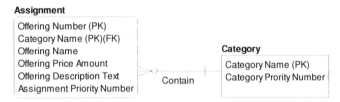

Rollup Denormalization:

Figure 10.3 Offering and Category logical with two different physical designs

ROLLDOWN DENORMALIZATION

Rolldown is the most common of the denormalization techniques. The parent entity in the relationship disappears, and all of the parent's columns and relationships are moved down to the child entity. You'll recall that the child entity is on the many side of the relationship and contains a foreign key back to the parent entity, which appears on the one side of the relationship.

In addition to choosing denormalization because of the need for faster retrieval time or for more user friendly structures, rolldown can be chosen in the following situations:

- **When you need to maintain the flexibility of the normalized model.** Folding the columns and relationships together using rolldown still allows one-to-one and one-to-many relationships to be stored (but not enforced in the database). In Figure 10.3, for example, we did not lose the flexibility that an **Offering** can belong to many **Categories**.

- **When you want to reduce development time and complexity.** Often there is a direct relationship between the number of tables and relationships on a model and the amount of effort it will take to develop the application. A developer will need to write code that jumps from one table to another to collect certain columns, and this can take time and add complexity. Denormalizing into fewer tables using rolldown means the columns and relationships from different entities now exist in the same entity. In Figure 10.3, for example, if the developer needs to retrieve both offering information and the category name, they can easily do so from the same entity, **Assignment**.

ROLLUP DENORMALIZATION

In rollup, the same column or group of columns is repeated two or more times in the same entity. Also known as an *array*, rollup requires making the number of times something can occur static. Recall that in 1NF we removed repeating groups; rollup means we are adding back in repeating groups. We had to decide in Figure 10.3, for example, that the maximum number of categories an offering can be assigned is three.

In addition to choosing denormalization because of the need for faster retrieval time or for more user friendly structures, repeating groups may be chosen in the following situations:

- **When it makes more sense to keep the parent entity instead of the child entity.** When the parent entity is going to be used more frequently than the child entity, or if there are rules and columns to preserve in the parent entity format, it makes more sense to keep the parent entity.

- **When an entity instance will never exceed the fixed number of columns added.** In Figure 10.3, we are only allowing up to three categories for an offering. If we had a fourth category for an offering, for example, how would we handle this?

STAR SCHEMA

Denormalization is a term that is applied exclusively to relational physical data models because you can't denormalize something unless it has already been normalized. However, denormalization techniques can be applied to dimensional models as well—you just can't use the term *denormalization*. So the relational term *rolldown*, for example, can still be applied to a dimensional model; we just need to use a different term like *flattening* or *collapsing*.

A star schema is the most common dimensional physical data model structure. The term *meter* from the dimensional logical data model is replaced with the term *fact table* on the dimensional physical data model. A star schema results when each set of tables that make up a dimension is flattened into a single table. The fact table is in the center of the model, and each of the dimensions relate to the fact table at the lowest level of detail. A star schema is relatively easy to create and implement, and it visually appears simplistic to both IT and the business.

Recall the dimensional data model example from Figure 10.2, repeated here in Figure 10.4.

A star schema is when each hierarchy is flattened into a single table. So on this star schema, **Customer** is flattened into **Account**, **Country** is flattened into **Region**, and **Year** is flattened into **Month**.

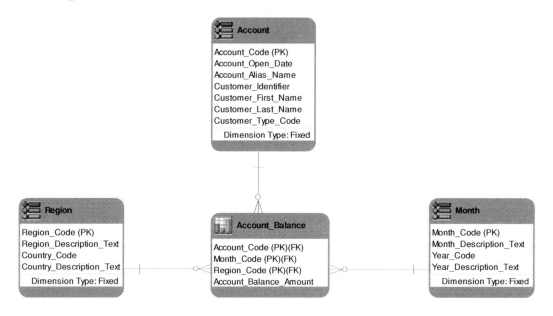

Figure 10.4 Financial dimensional PDM

VIEWS

A view is a virtual table. It is a dynamic "view" or window into one or more tables (or other views) where the actual data is stored. A view is defined by a SQL query that specifies how to collect data from its underlying tables. A SQL query is a request that a user (or reporting tool) makes of the database such as "Bring me back all **Customer IDs** where the **Customer** is 90 days or more behind in their bill payments." The difference between a query and a view, however, is that the instructions in a view are already prepared for the user (or reporting tool) and stored in the database as the definition of the view, whereas a query is not stored in the database and may need to be written each time a question is asked.

Figure 10.5 contains a view of **Assignment** and **Category** to create a simple way to display offerings along with their assigned categories.

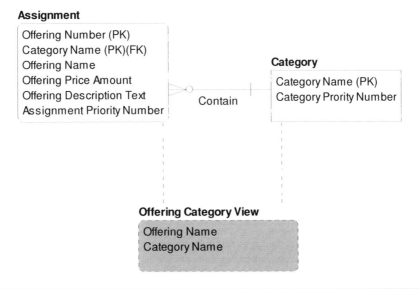

Figure 10.5 View creating a listing of offerings with their categories

Behind this view is the following SQL query needed to retrieve the authors and their titles:

```
CREATE VIEW "Offering Category View" AS
SELECT Assg."Offering Name", Ca."Category Name"
FROM Assignment Assg, Category Ca
WHERE Assg."Category Name" = Ca."Category Name"
ORDER BY Assg."Category Priority Number" DESC
```

Here is a sample of the results returned:

Offering Name	Category Name
Chocolate Sprinkles	Sprinkles
Chocolate Sprinkles	Chocolate
Rainbow Sprinkles	Sprinkles
Hot Fudge	Chocolate

INDEXING

An index is a value and a pointer to instances of that value in a table. In Chapter 5 we talked about and created primary keys, alternate keys, and inversion entries. Primary keys, alternate keys, and inversion entries are converted into indexes on the physical data model. Primary and alternate keys are converted into unique indexes, and inversion entries are converted into non-unique indexes.

PARTITIONING

Partitioning is when a table is split up into two or more tables. Vertical partitioning is when columns are split up, and horizontal is when rows are split up. It is common for both horizontal and vertical to be used together. That is, when splitting rows apart we in many cases learn that certain columns only belong with one set of rows.

Both vertical and horizontal partitioning are common techniques when building analytics systems. A table might contain a large number of columns and perhaps only a subset are volatile and change often, so this subset can be vertically partitioned into a separate table. Or we might have ten years of orders in a table, and to improve query performance we horizontally partition by year so that when queries are run within a given year the performance will be much faster.

Partitioning can be used as a reactive technique, meaning that even after an application goes live, the designer might choose to add partitioning after monitoring performance and space and determine that an improvement is needed.

EXERCISE 10: GETTING PHYSICAL WITH SUBTYPES

Subtyping is a powerful communication tool on the logical data model, because it allows the modeler to represent the similarities that exist between distinct business concepts to improve integration and data quality. As an example, refer to Figure 10.6 which contains these business rules:

- Each **Classroom** may be the location for one or many **Courses**.
- Each **Course** may be taught in one or many **Classrooms**.
- Each **Course** may be either a **Lecture** or a **Workshop**.
- Each **Lecture** is a **Course**.
- Each **Workshop** is a **Course**.
- Each **Workshop** may require as prerequisite one or many **Lectures**.
- Each **Lecture** must be the prerequisite for one **Workshop**.
- Each **Learning Track** must contain one or many **Lectures**.
- Each **Lecture** may belong to one **Learning Track**.
- Each **Learning Track** must contain one **Workshop**.
- Each **Workshop** may belong to one **Learning Track**.

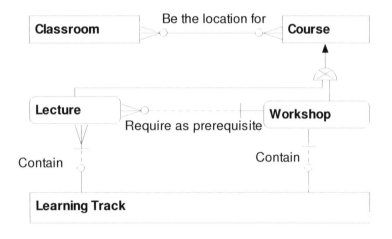

Figure 10.6 Course subtyping structure

Assume this is a logical data model (with attributes hidden to keep this example manageable). On the physical data model, we can replace this subtype symbol with one of three options:

- **Rolldown**. Remove the supertype entity and copy all of the attributes and relationships from the supertype to each of the subtypes.

- **Rollup**. Remove the subtypes and copy all of the attributes and relationships from each subtype to the supertype. Also add a type code to distinguish the subtypes.

- **Identity**. Convert the subtype symbol into a series of one-to-one relationships, connecting the supertype to each of the subtypes.

For this exercise, build all three physical options.

When you are done, refer to the answers section at the back of the book.

Key Points

- ✓ The physical data model builds upon the logical data model to produce a technical solution.

- ✓ Rolldown means the parent entity in the relationship disappears, and all of the parent's columns and relationships are moved down to the child entity.

- ✓ Rollup means the same column or group of columns is repeated two or more times in the same entity.

- ✓ A star schema results when each set of tables that make up a dimension is flattened into a single table.

- ✓ A view is a virtual table. It is a dynamic "view" or window into one or more tables (or other views) where the actual data is stored.

- ✓ An index is a value and a pointer to instances of that value in a table.

- ✓ Partitioning is when a table is split up into two or more tables. Vertical partitioning is when columns are split up, and horizontal is when rows are split up.

By now, you know the important role data modeling plays in application development, you know the components of a data model, and you know the five different types of data models. Now that we have all this data modeling knowledge, how can we improve the quality of our data modeling deliverables? Section IV focuses on improving data model quality through templates, the Data Model Scorecard, and better communication with businesspeople and the project team.

Chapter 11 goes through some useful templates for capturing and validating requirements. These templates will save time as well as improve the accuracy of the resulting data model.

Chapter 12 focuses on the Data Model Scorecard, a proven technique for validating data model quality. The quality of the data model directly impacts many characteristics of the resulting application, including stability and data quality.

Chapter 13 provides advice for the analyst and data modeler on working with other team members. Graeme Simsion has worked in the data modeling field for twenty-five years as a practitioner, teacher and researcher, and he shares his experiences on setting expectations, staying on track, and achieving closure.

CHAPTER 11
Which templates can help with capturing requirements?

Recycle, reuse
Easy to fill in templates
Consistency rules

There are a number of templates I use that save modeling time as well as improve the accuracy of the resulting data model. These tools are the focus of this chapter. You don't need to use every tool for every modeling effort—pick and choose the ones that make sense for your environment and the people you're working with.

The In-The-Know Template captures the people and documentation that can contribute and validate the data requirements. The Concept List is a compilation of the key concepts the business feels are important to capture, along with their definitions. The Family Tree is a spreadsheet that captures the source applications and other key metadata for each concept or attribute within the scope of our application.

IN-THE-KNOW TEMPLATE

The In-The-Know Template captures the people and documentation that can provide and validate the data requirements. It is a record of peoples' names and roles and contact information, as well as a list of where other important resources are located. For example, it contains the location of useful documentation for completing data modeling deliverables, such as business and functional requirements. Relying on memory instead of writing the locations down can lead to forgetting how to find the documents. Table 11.1 contains a sample In-The-Know Template.

Term	Resource	Type	Role / How used	Location / Contact
Customer	Tom Jones	Subject Matter Expert	Customer Reference Data Administrator	212-555-1212
	Customer classification list	Reference document	To validate and create new customer classifications	S:/customer/cust clsfn.xls
Item	Current Item Report	Report	To identify all current item information	www.item.com

Table 11.1 Sample In-The-Know Template

Here is a description on how each of these columns is used:

- **Term.** This is the concept name. You can take the list of concepts from a conceptual data model or the Concept List (the next technique discussed) and put them right into this column. Examples from Table 11.1 are **Customer** and **Item**.

- **Resource.** This is the source of the information. In this template, it is broad enough to be anything useful. It includes people, requirements documents, reports, etc. Be as specific as possible in this description column. If there is more than one resource for the same concept, use a separate row in the template for the additional resources. Examples from Table 11.1 are Tom Jones, Customer classification list, and Current Item Report.

- **Type.** Provides a general categorization of each of the resources. Because this template can be so generic, it is important to put each of the resources into the most appropriate category. Examples from Table 11.1 are Subject Matter Expert, Reference document, and Report. This is an optional category that is most useful when the In-The-Know Template is very large.

- **Role / How used.** This provides why the resource is valuable to this project. Why are we bothering to list this resource in this template? Be specific! Examples from Table 11.1 are Customer Reference Data Administrator, To validate and create new customer classifications, and To identify all current item information.

- **Location / Contact.** This column contains how to reach the resource. If the resource is a document, this column might contain the document's path name on a public drive or where to find it on a server or website. If the resource is a person, this column might contain the person's phone number or email address. Examples from Table 11.1 are 212-555-1212, S:/customer/custclsfn.xls, and www.item.com.

The In-The-Know Template captures the people and documentation that can provide and validate the data requirements. Having this information in a standard format accomplishes several goals:

- **Provides a handy and complete reference list.** This template is easy to read and provides all of the types of information that are necessary to identify people and documentation resources. Even years after the project is in production, this list could still be useful for functional or technical project questions.

- **Finds gaps or redundancy in your available list of resources.** This document will highlight any missing information. For example, if there is no available expert on item information, it will be very evident here. If you are missing a key reference document, you will notice it here and can raise it to management's attention.

- **Acts as a sign off document.** For example, if a person is identified as a resource for a particular concept, their management can be made aware of this and allocate their time accordingly. This way you will minimize the chances that your customer expert is pulled in another direction when you need their help.

CONCEPT LIST

The Concept List is a handy starting point if you feel it might be too much of a jump to start capturing high level business rules—that is, the relationships on a conceptual data model. The Concept List is a compilation of the key concepts the business feels are important to capture, without introducing data modeling notation. As your model develops, you might need to refine terms and definitions on the Concept List to keep them up-to-date and valuable. Table 11.2 shows a sample Concept List.

Name	Synonyms	Definition	Questions
Asset	Machine, Part, Capital, Stock, Wealth, Supplies	Something our company owns that is considered to be valuable.	Does this also include purchases we plan on making for the upcoming year?
Carrier	Trucking Company, Distributor, Transporter	A company that physically moves our products from one site to another site.	Does carrier include both company-owned carriers and externally-owned? Or just our own carriers?
Company	Corporation, Firm, Organization, Partnership	A business enterprise that serves a purpose to society and the economy.	Are our business units or subsidiaries considered separate companies within a larger company, or do we just have one company?
Contract	Order, Promotion, Agreement, Invoice, Bill of Lading, Bill of Materials, Purchase Order, Policy, Statement	A document containing the terms and conditions around the purchase or creation of product.	What is the difference between a transaction and a contract? Which happens first?

Table 11.2 Sample Concept List

Here is a description of each of the columns:

- **Name**. Name contains the most common term for each concept. Ideally, this will be an enterprise-wide agreed-upon name for this concept. Subject areas are listed alphabetically by name.

- **Synonyms**. Synonyms are a great place to list aliases for this term. When there is more than one name for the same concept, listing all of the names under Synonyms is a step towards reaching a single name and definition. This column also includes those words that are more specific to a particular industry, or those terms that are at a more detailed level than the concept. For example, **Order** in this column is a more specific term for the **Contract** concept.

- **Definition**. Definition contains a brief description of each of the concepts. The basic definition is designed to be generic enough to be easily customizable, yet detailed enough to provide value.

- **Questions**. Questions contain some queries or comments that might be worthwhile addressing when refining your concept definitions. This last column can spark lively discussion and debate, resulting in a more solid concept definition. Your goal for these questions is to more clearly articulate the definition of a concept by answering what that concept does and does not include.

The Concept List is a very simple tool which accomplishes a number of important goals:

- **Creates a high-level understanding of the application's concepts.** After completing this checklist, you and the rest of the project team will clearly understand each concept and know what is within the scope of the application. When you start the modeling process, you will already know the concepts and only have to add the relationships between these concepts to complete the conceptual model.

- **Gets your project team 'out of the weeds'.** This is useful when your project team wants to start off the modeling phase by diving directly into the attributes. In these situations, it can be very easy to miss key concepts and accidentally leave out required information. Starting the application analysis by listing attributes creates a narrow and incomplete view of the project's requirements. In order to step back and really understand the scope of the application, your team can appreciate the broad and complete picture through a conceptual view.

- **Facilitates entity and attribute names and definitions.** Having solid names and definitions at the conceptual level makes it easier to develop names and definitions at more detailed levels. If we have a standard name and very good definition for Customer, for example, we can name and define the entities **Customer Location** and **Customer Association**, and the attributes **Customer Last Name** and **Customer Type Code** more easily.

- **Initiates rapport with the project team and business users.** Completing the Concept List as a group is a very good first data modeling task for you and the rest of the team. It is a quick win, meaning it is not usually very difficult to complete, yet has big payoffs. It can improve everyone's understanding of the new application's content at a high-level, as well as help build rapport with the project team.

FAMILY TREE

The Family Tree is a spreadsheet that captures source information and other key descriptive information for each concept or attribute within the scope of our application. The greater the number of source systems, the more valuable the Family Tree. The Family Tree works especially well when our application is a data mart, because this tool can capture which information currently exists in the data warehouse and which applications we will require new information from.

Keeping the sourcing information neatly organized within a spreadsheet makes validation much easier than sifting through pages in a requirements document. A spreadsheet is an extremely unambiguous way to represent the sourcing requirements. Once the concept or attribute source is validated and agreed upon, the Family Tree is still useful as a reference. Long after the application is developed and in production, people will still need to refer to this information. Table 11.3 contains an example of a Family Tree at a conceptual level.

Here is a description of each of the columns in this spreadsheet:

- **Name**. This column contains the names of all the concepts or attributes within the application. If a concept or attribute is left out of this document, there is a good chance that it will not be in the data model. Name needs to be specified on both the "From Here" and "To Arrive

Here" sections of the spreadsheet because there may be different names for each. For example on Table 11.3, **Item** on the "From Here" side and **Product** on the "To Arrive Here" side.

- **Source**. This column contains the name of the application that provides the data for each concept or attribute. Note that a source application is not just limited to a database, but can also be a file or a spreadsheet. A very important question to answer at this point is "How far should I go back?" That is, should we list all of the source applications until we reach the point where a user is typing the information in? Or should we just go back to the immediate source? My advice is to continue following the concept or attribute upstream until you arrive at a reliable and accurate source for this concept or attribute, and then stop. On Table 11.3 for example, in order to get **Associate**, we need to go back to the data warehouse, which stores **Associate** as **Party**.

- **Definition**. Just as we saw with the Name column, on this tree, we can have multiple definitions of a single concept or attribute. However, there is also a slim chance that one of the source systems might have a definition slightly different from the enterprise definition. On Table 11.3 for example, the definition of Item on the "From Here" side of the spreadsheet is much broader than the definition of Product on the "To Arrive Here" side of the spreadsheet.

- **History**. The History column under the source set of columns is the number of years of history the system maintains on this concept or attribute. Luckily, in our example on Table 11.3, the history needs can all be met. The number of years required on the "To Arrive Here" side is always less than the number of years available on the "From Here" side. If we want more history than is available in our source system, we have an issue. Working with our users, we may be able to agree that in the beginning, there will be less history, and over time, the history will accumulate to the level they are requiring. Finding this history gap early catches a potentially serious problem before much time has been invested in the project and helps set the users' expectations. This column is optional for operational applications, but mandatory for business intelligence applications.

From Here				To Arrive Here		
Name	Source	Definition	History	Name	Definition	History
Customer	Customer Reference Database	The recipient and purchaser of our products.	10	Customer	The recipient and purchaser of our products.	3
Order	Order Entry	A contract to buy a quantity of product at a specified price.	4	Order	A contract to buy a quantity of product at a specified price.	3
Item	Item Reference Database	Anything we buy, sell, stock, move, or make. Any manufactured or purchased part, material, component, assembly, or product.	10	Product	Anything we sell.	3
Party	Data Warehouse	A person or company that is important to our business in some way.	5	Associate	A person who is employed in a full or part time capacity by our company, to perform a service or function to our company.	3
Time	Data Warehouse	A measurable length of seconds, minutes, hours, days, weeks, months or years. Can include both fiscal and Julian time measurements.	10	Calendar	A measurable length of days.	3

Table 11.3 Sample Conceptual Family Tree

Additional types of descriptive information may be included in the Family Tree, especially at an attribute level. For example, it can contain formatting information such as attribute length and domain.

The Family Tree has several objectives:

- **Captures each concept's or attribute's source information.** The Family Tree contains each of the applications that play a role in transporting and shaping the content of each of the concepts or attributes.

- **Estimates work effort.** Before starting development, you can gauge pretty accurately how much effort it would take to get the information required. You can judge how many applications are involved and the impact each application will have on your development and vice versa. This allows you to create an estimate of the effort it will take to bring this new information into the application.

- **Identifies sourcing issues early.** Let's say your users want three years of history for **Customer** and by filling in the Family Tree, you realize that the source system only keeps one year of **Customer** history. This is a problem that you have discovered with a minimal amount of analysis and time. Identifying problems like this one early on is a great benefit of this tool. It takes a proactive approach to sourcing issues.

EXERCISE 11: BUILDING THE TEMPLATE

What role in your organization is responsible for completing the Family Tree? At what point in the development process should this template be completed?

When you are done, refer to the answers section at the back of the book.

Key Points

- ✓ The In-The-Know Template captures the people and documentation that can provide and validate the data requirements.

- ✓ The Concept List is a compilation of the key concepts the business feels are important to capture, without introducing data modeling notation.

- ✓ The Family Tree is a spreadsheet that captures the source applications and other key metadata for each concept or attribute within the scope of our application.

Pay now, not later
Get the data model right
Sleep better at night

A frequently overlooked aspect of data quality management is that of data model quality. We often build data models quickly, in the midst of a development project, and with the singular goal of database design. Yet the implications of those models are far-reaching and long-lasting. They affect the structure of implemented data, the ability to adapt to change, understanding of and communication about data, definition of data quality rules, and much more. In many ways, high-quality data begins with high-quality data models. Therefore, because a good data model can lead to a good application, and similarly, a bad data model can lead to a bad application, we need an objective way of measuring what is good or bad about the model. After reviewing hundreds of data models, I formalized the criteria I have been using into what I call the Data Model Scorecard. This chapter will briefly explain the Data Model Scorecard and its ten categories.

For a more detailed description of the Data Model Scorecard, please refer to my book, *Data Model Scorecard: Applying the Industry Standard on Data Model Quality*.

DATA MODEL SCORECARD EXPLAINED

The Data Model Scorecard is a proactive approach to measuring the quality of a data model. The Scorecard has four important characteristics:

- **Highlights not just areas for improvement but also strengths**. The Scorecard not only makes recommendations on areas for improvement, but highlights strengths, giving specific examples of what was done using best design practices. For example, in the same

Scorecard report below on the data model for the HAL application, there is a list of both strengths and areas for improvement. Point #25 on this report acknowledges the strength that the model has a perfect balance of abstraction. Abstraction is the use of generic concepts such as "Party" and "Event." Point #125 however captures an area of improvement, namely that when a surrogate key is used, an alternate key should be identified such as on a business key or source system identifier.

Data Model Scorecard review of HAL application
…
25. "There is a perfect balance of abstraction on the model because…"
…
125. "A surrogate key requires an alternate key. On this entity you might consider the alternate key to be…"

- **Provides external perspective**. Team rapport remains intact because you, as the reviewer, are not directly criticizing your colleague's data model. Instead, this objective and external scale indicates areas for improvement. The Scorecard uses a points system and several metrics for measuring model quality. Using the Scorecard avoids the emotional situations of having one colleague criticize another colleague's work. Discussions starting off with an emotionally charged phrase such as "I hate what you did there…" usually don't end well. Better to say something like "The Scorecard recommends we make this change to the model…" I have been in extremely fraught data model reviews (even to the point of having someone leave the room crying!), and the Scorecard takes a lot of the emotion out of the equation.

- **Offers straightforward review approach**. The scorecard was designed for even those new to modeling to critique their own models and the models of their colleagues. Follow the approach outlined in this chapter and you will find yourself providing feedback on data models even if you are not an experienced data modeler! If you are an experienced data modeler, you can use the Scorecard to organize your own thinking in reviewing data models.

- **Supports all types of models**. The Scorecard is designed to be used for all model levels of detail: conceptual, logical, and physical. It also supports relational, dimensional, and NoSQL model schemes.

SCORECARD TEMPLATE

Table 12.1 contains the template I complete for each model review.

#	Category	Total score	Model score	%	Comments
1	How well does the model capture the requirements?	15			
2	How complete is the model?	15			
3	How well does the model match its scheme?	10			
4	How structurally sound is the model?	15			
5	How well does the model leverage generic structures?	10			
6	How well does the model follow naming standards?	5			
7	How well has the model been arranged for readability?	5			
8	How good are the definitions?	10			
9	How consistent is the model with the enterprise?	5			
10	How well does the metadata match the data?	10			
	TOTAL SCORE	100			

Table 12.1 Data Model Scorecard template

Each of the ten categories has a total score that relates to the value your organization places on the question. Because we want to express the result as a percentage, the total must equal 100. The model score column contains the results of a particular model review. For example, if a model received 10 on Category 1 ("How well does the model capture the requirements?"), then that is what would go in this column. The % column stores the model score in category divided by the total score in category. For example, receiving 10 out of 15 would lead to 66%. The comments column contains any pertinent information to explain the score in more details or to capture the action items required to fix the model. You may find it useful to always have at least a summary statement in the comments column. Even if there are no issues for a particular category, we can still summarize that the model did well in this category. The last row contains the total score, tallied up for each of the columns to arrive at an overall score for a particular model review.

SCORECARD SUMMARY

Here is a summary of each of these ten categories:

1. **How well does the model capture the requirements?** Here we ensure that the data model represents the requirements. If there is a requirement to capture order information, in this category we check the model to make sure it captures order information. If there is a requirement to view **Student Count** by **Semester** and **Major**, in this category we make sure the data model supports this query.

2. **How complete is the model?** Here completeness means two things: completeness of requirements and completeness of metadata. Completeness of requirements means that each requirement that has been requested appears on the model (note we don't check for whether the requirement has been modeled correctly, which is the first category), as well as that the data model only contains what is being asked for and nothing extra. Sometimes we may add structures to the model anticipating they will be used in the near future; we note these sections of the model too during the review because it is always easy to model something and may be hard to deliver and may impact the entire project if the modeler includes something that was never asked for. We need to consider the likely cost of including a future requirement in the case that it never eventuates. Completeness of metadata means that all

of the descriptive information surrounding the model is present as well; for example, if we are reviewing a physical data model, we would expect formatting and nullability to appear on the data model.

3. **How well does the model match its scheme?** Here we ensure that the model type (conceptual, logical, or physical—and then either relational, dimensional, or NoSQL) of the model being reviewed matches the definition for this type of model. The conceptual defines the scope and captures the business need, the logical is technology-independent and represents a business solution, and the physical is technology-dependent and tuned for performance, security, and development tool constraints, capturing the technical solution. The relational perspective captures business rules, the dimensional perspective captures business questions, and the NoSQL perspective captures how non-RDBMS technologies store data such as in a document or graph.

4. **How structurally sound is the model?** Here we validate the design practices employed to build the model. Assume you were comfortable reading an architectural blueprint and somebody shared their house blueprint with you. If there was a toilet drawn in the middle of the kitchen, a room with no doorway, or a garage drawn in the attic, you would probably catch it. The data model is to a database as a blueprint is to a house. Therefore, you would catch anything structurally incorrect on a data model. For example, a null primary key would be corrected to be required instead of optional.

5. **How well does the model leverage generic structures?** Here we confirm an appropriate use of abstraction. Going from **Customer Location** to a more generic **Location**, for example, allows the design to more easily handle other types of locations such as warehouses and distribution centers. However, it comes with the high price of obscurity and difficulty of enforcing rules. Abstraction must therefore be applied only in situations where it makes the most sense: where flexibility is more important than usability. So we tend to see abstraction more on data warehouse data models over analytical data models, for example.

6. **How well does the model follow naming standards?** Here we ensure correct and consistent naming standards have been applied to the data model. We focus on naming standard structure, term, and style. Structure means that the proper building blocks are being used for entities, relationships, and attributes. For example, a building block for an attribute would be the subject of the attribute such as "Customer" or "Product." Term means that the proper name is given to the attribute or entity. Term also includes proper spelling and abbreviation. Style means that the appearance, such as upper case or camelback case, is consistent with standard practices.

7. **How well has the model been arranged for readability?** Here we ensure the data model is easy to read. This question is not the most important of the ten categories. However, if your model is hard to read, you may not accurately address the more important categories on the scorecard. Placing parent entities above their child entities, displaying related entities together, and minimizing relationship line length all improve model readability.

8. **How good are the definitions?** Here we ensure the definitions are clear, complete, and correct. Clarity means that a reader can understand the meaning of a term by reading the definition only once. Completeness means that the definition is at the appropriate level of detail and that it includes all the necessary components such as derivations, synonyms, exceptions, and examples. Correctness means that the definition completely matches what the term means and is consistent with the rest of the business.

9. **How consistent is the model with the enterprise?** Here we ensure the structures on the data model are represented in a broad and consistent context, so that one set of terminology and rules can be spoken in the organization. Ideally we would compare the data model being reviewed with an enterprise data model.

10. **How well does the metadata match the data?** Here we confirm the model and the actual data that will be stored within the resulting structures are consistent with each other. Does the column

Customer_Last_Name really contain the customer's last name, for example? The Data category is designed to reduce these surprises and help ensure the structures on the model match the data these structures will be holding.

SCORECARD EXAMPLE

Following is an example of an actual Scorecard report I created based on a recent data model review:

#	Category	Total score	Model score	%	Comments
1.	How well does the model capture the requirements?	15	14	93%	Revisit some AKs
2.	How complete is the model?	15	15	100%	Legacy system mapping
3.	How well does the model match its scheme?	10	10	100%	Lots of processing attributes
4.	How structurally sound is the model?	15	10	66%	Null AKs
5.	How well does the model leverage generic structures?	10	10	100%	Perfect use of abstraction
6.	How well does the model follow naming standards?	5	4	80%	Great standard for table naming
7.	How well has the model been arranged for readability?	5	4	80%	Incorporate a conceptual data model
8.	How good are the definitions?	10	9	90%	Very comprehensive definitions
9.	How consistent is the model with the enterprise?	5	5	100%	Great rapport with business
10.	How well does the metadata match the data?	10	10	100%	Handles changing natural account numbers
	TOTAL SCORE	**100**	**91**		

The model that was reviewed in this example received a score of 91. I share this Scorecard report with you because 91 is the highest score I have ever given in a data model review. I believe that lower scores tend to stimulate action. Nobody wants to get a low score, so a low score traditionally receives a rapid response and the model is quickly corrected along with a request to rescore. For example, if someone gives you a data model to review that is missing definitions and you give the model zero in the definitions category, you will most likely get a very quick response from the modeler saying the definitions will arrive shortly. It is good to be a strict grader, as the end result is a higher quality data model and therefore a higher quality application!

Note on this report that category 4 was a strong area for improvement and categories 6 and 7 also contain areas for improvement. There was a 50 page document that accompanied this Scorecard. This document explained the results in detail. Both strengths and areas for improvement were explained in detail through a complete set or representative set of examples. For example, Category 4 lost points because this model was missing some alternate keys. In the accompanying document, those entities missing alternate keys were listed as well as those entities with suspect alternate keys.

You can use the Scorecard on any of your projects—it is not proprietary. In fact, I would love every organization on the planet to use the Scorecard! Here is the reference to include:

EXERCISE 12: DETERMINING THE MOST CHALLENGING SCORECARD CATEGORY

Which of the Scorecard categories do you think would be the most challenging to grade, and why?

When you are done, refer to the answers section at the back of the book.

Key Points

✓ The Data Model Scorecard is a proactive approach to measuring the quality of a data model.

✓ Applying the Scorecard early in the modeling process saves rework later and increases the chances that your comments on the model will be incorporated.

✓ You can use the Scorecard on any of your projects—it is not proprietary.

CHAPTER 13
How can we work effectively with others?

Set expectations
Stay on track, achieve closure
Strong relationships

By Graeme Simsion

Graeme Simsion worked in the data modeling field for twenty-five years as a practitioner, teacher and researcher. He is the author of *Data Modeling Essentials*, now in its third edition, and *Data Modeling Theory and Practice*. He now focuses on teaching consulting and facilitation skills, drawing on his experience as CEO of a successful business and IT consultancy. In this chapter, he shares his experiences of setting expectations, staying on track, and achieving closure.

RECOGNIZING PEOPLE ISSUES

For some years, I taught an advanced class in data modeling. In the opening session, I would ask the delegates – most of them very experienced modelers – to nominate their biggest challenge. Overwhelmingly, their responses were about working with others: persuading business and technical people of the value of data modeling; getting access to business stakeholders and communicating effectively with them; building an effective working relationship with the database administration team.

Curiously, they were then not always enthusiastic about devoting much of the class to dealing with these problems. There was a sense that they were inevitable, and that data modelers could not do much to prevent or resolve them. It's easier to stick to the technical issues.

This chapter takes the position that:

- Many of the most serious challenges you face in data modeling will be "people issues" or, if you prefer, "political issues"

- These challenges can be addressed in a disciplined way, largely by process rather than through ill-defined "people skills"

- Most modelers can substantially improve their performance in this area by adopting just a few basic principles and practices

The word *basic* in the third point deserves a comment. Much of what I cover in this chapter is "common sense", detailed in innumerable books on project management, psychology, sales, and personal development. The only originality I claim is in putting it in the context of data modeling. But as you read, ask yourself not only whether you agree with the recommended approaches, but whether you consistently apply them in your day-to-day work. The step many modelers need to take is to commit to working in a way that they know intellectually is right, but which gets lost in the pressures and emotions of the immediate situation.

This chapter falls logically into three sections: broadly, *setting expectations*, *staying on track*, and *achieving closure*. The first is the most important: in my experience failure to clearly establish mutual expectations is the most common reason for the failure of assignments both within and outside the data modeling sphere.

In looking at these "soft" challenges, I recognize that data modelers do more than create data models. They may be asked to review existing models, advise on modeling approaches, evaluate tools … In much of this work, they will find themselves effectively (or actually) working as consultants, providing services to a client rather than simply working to direction. Specialist data modelers may be part of a common team (an internal or external consultancy), with its own objectives above and beyond those of the project team. Consulting brings its own relationship management challenges, and we will look at these along the way.

SETTING EXPECTATIONS

A successful data modeling engagement needs to be based on a set of expectations that are understood and agreed upon by all stakeholders. Easy to say, but in the haste to get moving, we can forget the lessons from our programmer brethren (and indeed the advice we would give on the database side) and fail to put a proper specification of work in place. We will look at some key questions to ask – and who to ask – in establishing such a specification, but before we bury ourselves in the detail, we need to establish the big picture.

UNDERSTANDING CONTEXT

It's sometimes called "asking the next-higher question." "Why are we doing this? What does the client / project manager / sponsor want it for? And, consequently, exactly what sort of deliverable is needed to serve that purpose?" I would suggest that failure to understand and address this *context* in which work is being performed is the single greatest cause of problems in data modeling assignments.

A simple example: a team was assembled to undertake a classic data mining project, looking at an operational database for "interesting correlations". The highly-qualified team included a data modeler to reverse engineer the database, as well as a statistician to interpret results. After some preliminary work, they produced a steady stream of "interesting correlations", but the client remained consistently unimpressed. At this point, I became involved. My first question to the "difficult" client was, "why are you doing this?" The response: "Because our organization has been criticized in a public report, and we wanted to know whether any of the claims in the report could be refuted by our operational data." It took no more than an hour with a copy of the report and a highlighting pen to identify the statements that might be corroborated or refuted by the data, and only a day for the data mining team to produce answers – to the satisfaction of the client.

In the review that followed, the mining team was quick to point out that the client had not explained the reason for the work, that they'd never heard of the report, and that the work actually required wasn't data mining anyway! I also suspect that having been given a brief to do exactly the sort of work they found professionally satisfying, they were not inclined to ask too many questions.

In data modeling at the project level, an understanding of context is essential in establishing quality, cost and timing requirements. The two most common complaints about data modelers are that they are impractical and that they take too long. I'm well aware of the defenses to these accusations, having used them many times myself, but we have to acknowledge the perceptions. And they are *context* issues. Behind the complaints is the suspicion that some data modelers are more concerned with the intrinsic quality of the model than with its contribution to the success of the project: "the operation was a success but the patient died".

Like other professionals, data modelers want to produce high-quality results – but need to remember that quality is *fitness for purpose* rather than an absolute standard. We are well aware of the consequences of substandard models, but are often less aware of how to compromise (and indeed are sometimes not willing to compromise) in order to meet overall project goals. If the project is time-critical, then timely delivery may be more critical than intrinsic quality factors. We should also remember that data modeling has no natural end. As with any design product, a data model can always be improved – indefinitely. It's easy to be caught in the perfection trap: pursuing the perfect "correct" model when all we are doing is refining a design beyond the point of worthwhile returns.

At least in applications development, we have a broad idea of the purpose of the data model. In strategic work, such as development of an enterprise data model, we cannot take even this for granted. Time and again I have seen enterprise models developed without a precise understanding of how they will be used. The result is frequently a model with unnecessary detail, or perhaps unfamiliar structures that do not sit easily with an organization's strategy of buying off-the-shelf software. Some advocates of enterprise models will argue that they need to be developed in "excruciating detail" - fine, as long as we have established exactly how and by whom that expensive detail is going to be used.

Remember – there is no such thing as a good data model independent of its purpose. Data modeling takes place in the context of a larger project, and will ultimately be judged by how well it contributes to that project's success.

IDENTIFYING THE STAKEHOLDERS

In the next subsection, we will look at some techniques for establishing expectations in more detail. But whose expectations? A common mistake in consulting is to identify a person or team as "the client" only to find at the end of the assignment that other stakeholders' needs have not been met. The following list of potential stakeholders and some of their likely expectations is a useful starting point.

- The *database designer* is a key "hands on" user of the final model. Many times I have seen data models developed without any serious preliminary discussion with the DBA. The model is handed over on the due date – and then the arguments start. The model is too generic, too hard to understand, won't perform. Setting – and arguing – the evaluation criteria at the outset, before substantial work has been done, can substantially reduce this risk.

- The *process developers,* from business analysts and process designers to programmers and testers, will need to be able to understand and work with the model. As in the case of the DBA, we need to understand what they expect of the model.

- More broadly, the *users* of whatever we are producing – be it an enterprise model, a review, a reverse-engineered database. We need to identify, at least at a group level, those who will be affected by any change that will result from our work.

- The *project manager* and *sponsors,* who have authorized the funding of the total package of work or the data modeling component, will have their own expectations. Our basic questions to them are: Why have you asked for this? How do you plan to use it? Budgets and timelines may have some flexibility – or not. And the data modeling component may be seen as worthy of additional effort to get the best result – or it may not.

- *Subject matter experts* who will be concerned about the time required of them and their staff.

- *Technical stakeholders* are people outside the project who require adherence to standards – perhaps use of particular tools or platforms. External consultants are likely to have to meet the expectations of a purchasing department, as embodied in a legal contract.

- The *consultancy manager* is typically your line manager – perhaps the head of a central data modeling or enterprise architecture group. They may have their own agenda and expectations – typically, that work conforms to enterprise standards and that documentation is added to a central repository. If you're working for an external consultancy, there is likely to be an agenda of building a reputation and relationships that will lead to further work.

There is nothing novel in the above analysis of stakeholders and needs; the challenge is to act on it and actually establish these and any other stakeholders' needs at the outset of the exercise. This is also a good time to think about the level of involvement that these players should have in the work. One of the great lessons of change management is that people will work very hard to implement something that they have helped to design – and conversely will be resistant to ideas and designs imposed upon them. Perhaps it's worth involving that "difficult" DBA in the modeling effort – right from the start.

ASKING KEY QUESTIONS

At the outset of a data modeling assignment, we need to establish the expectations of all of the stakeholders (clients). We recognize that these may change as work proceeds, and will commit to monitoring and documenting such changes. Our motto should be "no surprises".

Here are a few questions that can help clarify expectations, both in terms of deliverables and method of working.

- **What does the final product look like?** The client should understand *in concrete terms* what they will be getting. Words like *architecture, model, strategy,* and even *report* are ambiguous, and we can have no confidence that a client who signs up for one of these has the same thing in mind as us. If we can't show them the deliverable from a previous exercise as a sample, we will need to generate a sample in an early project phase. Until the client has seen and agreed to a concrete example, we cannot claim to understand their expectations. In the case of a report, it makes sense to outline section headings and approximate number of pages as indications of depth and effort.

- **What does "success" look like to the stakeholder?** Sometimes the answer, to our surprise, is very different from our understanding, although the stakeholder is unlikely to tell us directly. You might be brought in to "improve" or "coach" a team, or review their performance, sponsored by a more senior manager. The team or individuals may take a defensive position, and aim to demonstrate that their current practices could not be improved upon - "success" in their terms.

- **Who will direct the work day-to-day?** Is the client interested only in the deliverable, or do they want to direct the process? This is likely to affect financial arrangements – fixed price or "time and materials".

- **Who is formally authorized to accept the deliverable?** Most of the time, one or more of your stakeholders will formally accept the deliverable. Make sure you know who this is and have them involved in the process as much as possible to ensure this signoff is a formality without any surprises.

- **How will disputes be resolved?** If we can envisage (say) the DBA refusing to accept our model (hopefully something we establish before the deadline), we should discuss the possibility in advance and agree on the approach. We can then work with that in mind, and if a dispute does arise, the client will at least be reassured that we anticipated it.

- **Whose name will go on the deliverable?** As a consultant, I encourage the client to own the deliverable with my role being to help them develop it. This makes handover much easier – and makes rejection a great deal less likely!

- **What provision will be made for follow-up?** Particularly if the client will be charged (internally or externally) for further work, it is much easier to sell this at the outset, when it is likely to be perceived as responsible planning, than at the end, when it may be seen as an attempt to secure further work – possibly requiring new expenditure approvals.

PACKAGING IT UP

The end-result of this initial establishment of expectations – typically taking a week or two – should be a detailed plan for your component of the work, integrated, of course, with the project plan. It is critical that this becomes the *sole* documentation of expectations – overriding or specifically incorporating any previous promises. Many assignments begin with a conversation and an informal agreement – and clients have been known to bring such conversations up at the end of the assignment.

The plan should include a schedule of interviews. Many an assignment has been held up by key people being unavailable. If this happens, we want to have the leverage (or at least excuse) of a written commitment.

STAYING ON TRACK

Having established expectations, our prime task is to devote our efforts to meeting them. Note that I say *meeting* rather than repeating the conventional wisdom that we should aim to exceed expectations. Generally, exceeding expectations means doing more than what we agreed to do – and someone has to pay for that. If you think that more should be done to create an acceptable product (and this is not an uncommon situation) then raise the extra work with the client and seek to have it included in the agreed plan. If the client isn't prepared to sign up for it, advise them clearly of the consequences – then get on with delivering what the client wants. As a participant in my class observed "most of the time, just meeting expectations exceeds expectations".

As work proceeds, we also need to keep our eyes open for any changes to expectations, and deal with problems as they arise. In this section, I suggest a few practices that can help keep you on track, and some approaches to dealing with problems – in particular "people problems".

FOLLOWING GOOD PRACTICES

In the spirit of Stephen Covey's *Seven Habits of Highly Effective People*, here are seven "habits" or practices that can help keep an assignment on track.

- **Habit 1: Work close to the client.** We often have a choice as to where to locate ourselves: at the client's place of work, back at our "home" desk, or at our real homes. Whenever possible, I choose the client's place of work, even though it may be less convenient. Clients like to see us working – some will assume that if we're not on site, we'll be distracted by other tasks. I can keep my ear to the ground, test ideas informally, and build some relationships with the client team. If I want to build joint ownership of the project and the deliverables (and I generally do!), then being physically close makes it much easier.

- **Habit 2: Keep in touch with all of the stakeholders.** We need to stay in touch with all stakeholders, in particular the sponsor and technical buyers, to ensure their expectations are being met and have not changed. Unless we explicitly schedule meetings, chances are we will ignore the people who are not providing direct input to our task – until the end of the assignment, when they appear from the shadows. "Sure", we say to the sponsor, that's what we originally agreed, but we've persuaded the design team to move a long way from that..." Unfortunately, the sponsor has not made the journey with us.

- **Habit 3: Support the high-level relationship.** A key factor in the perceived success of a consulting assignment is the quality of the highest level relationship between the consulting organization and the client organization (which may of course be divisions of the same business). In other words, your boss should be in touch with the client's boss. It's your job to facilitate this; tell your boss when the time is right for a lunch or a coffee and keep him or her up to date so that a phone call from the client's boss doesn't come as a rude surprise.

- **Habit 4: Organize real progress meetings.** A key goal of regular progress meetings should be to "sign off" work performed so far, so that we eliminate the risk of being off track for a significant time. When the client explodes "this isn't what we asked for!" I want to be able to say "At last week's progress meeting we agreed we were on track, so at worst we've wasted a week…"   Achieving this isn't simple – but it's possible.

- **Habit 5: Listen.** When I ask other consultants to share their most important lessons, much of their advice boils down to "listen". As experts and / or consultants, we are tempted to keep justifying our presence by offering advice, "adding value", and generally pontificating, when what the client wants is help taking their own plans and ideas forward. Salespeople will tell you that they have to let the potential client speak, because not speaking means not buying. The same applies to selling ideas.

- **Habit 6: Take time out.** Stephen Covey would say "sharpen the saw", based on the old story about the lumberjack who was too busy cutting down the tree to do that. But there's more to it than just improving your skills. If you are working eighty hours a week, I guarantee you will have lost perspective. You can do without that for a little while (but make sure you get help with any decisions), but as a specialist, it is critical that you can see your work in context and offer objective advice. Consultants should not spend all their time with one client: there are past clients to follow up, prospective clients to woo, a "home" team to stay in touch with. Most importantly, you need time out to reflect on your experiences, on what has worked and what hasn't, and how you can incorporate the learning into your future consulting behaviour.

- **Habit 7: Keep a diary.** At the end of every consulting day, I write notes for myself, including working hours, key events, and reflections. It forces me to reflect on my work, supporting Habit 6, when the pressures of the consulting day are over. Occasionally a client will ask "what have you been doing for the last month?" and occasionally I'll ask myself the same question! The diary usually provides a reassuring answer.

DEALING WITH PROBLEMS – AND PROBLEM PEOPLE

Inevitably, problems will arise – technical problems and people problems. Regardless of the nature of the problem, there are some general principles that can be applied:

- **Establish whose problem it is – or at least who is accountable for solving it.** If it's someone else's problem that affects your work, focus on finding ways of working around the problem rather than taking it on yourself – and getting in the way of the person responsible.

- **Take time out.** Having gained an understanding of the problem, and shown your willingness to help, find some space to reflect on it, away from the pressure and emotion of the situation – especially if you're responsible for solving it.

- **Keep it in perspective – and help everyone else to do the same.** As an expert, you are expected to be professional. Keep emotions out of it, terminating angry exchanges if necessary or just staying cool. Think about the impact at the next higher level – and discuss it with someone operating at that level. A year or two down the road, you'll wonder why you bothered losing sleep.

- **Get help.** Just explaining the problem to a peer can help put it in perspective – and of course may put you on the way to a solution. If you are part of a central team or consultancy, discuss it with your manager. As a consulting manager, I used to tell consultants that the greatest consulting sin was failure to put your hand up and ask for help.

- **Assume rationality until proven otherwise.** When people are behaving in a way we don't like, a natural inclination is to put it down to personality defects. Unfortunately, we are most unlikely to be able to change personalities. In my experience, however, most behavior in the workplace has a rational basis in furthering the person's goals. If you understand these goals, you can often work out what is going on. Or, working in the other direction, you can ask "under what circumstances might a rational person do this?"

- **Know your own sensibilities and vulnerabilities.** Most of us have "buttons" that are pushed by certain people or circumstances. "Know thyself" is the watchword here, so we can recognize when the problem is (at least partly) ourselves. If you know your (Jungian-based) Myers-Briggs type[2] and its implications, you may find yourself smiling when you recognize a clash that can be explained by that model. For example, Types N and S clash over levels of detail; Types J and P over the need for closure.

- **Keep the focus on the path forward.** When things go wrong, it's natural to look for someone to blame – especially if you're confident it's someone else's fault. I strongly suggest that if you must do this, you leave it until the problem is solved – which is usually the greater priority. And once it is solved, the actual impact is known, replacing fear of unbounded consequences.

- **Keep it in the kitchen.** Keep any disputes that arise within your "home" team within that team, just as, if you were hosting a dinner party, you would not expose your guests to arguments about the cooking.

- **Learn from the experience.** When the problem has gone – solved, bypassed, perhaps ignored – convene a meeting with at least one other person, ideally from your "home" team, and reflect on the experience. Lessons learned from mistakes are lessons remembered, so it's worth making the most of them.

ACHIEVING CLOSURE

Most of us have had the experience of working hard to get a model or report completed on time, and feeling more than a little anxious about how it will be received. Its presentation becomes a big event: will the work be accepted as it

---

[2] Myers, Isabel Briggs with Peter B. Myers (1980, 1995). *Gifts Differing: Understanding Personality Type*. Mountain View, CA: Davies-Black Publishing. ISBN 0-89106-074-X.

stands, will the client want changes, or will they take a deep breath and begin, uncomfortably, "you've obviously put a lot of work into this, but..."?

In a well-managed assignment, this situation should not arise. The final deliverable should be just one more step in a journey that all stakeholders have taken or at least followed. If there are problems, they should be with the last increment of work.

We can do a few things to facilitate a tidy closure. Not surprisingly, most of them need to be done throughout the assignment rather than at the end.

If we can define the end of the assignment as a hand-over rather than a sign-off, the question to the client changes from "do we need to do more to make it right?" to "are you able to take it from here?". Practically and psychologically, it will be easier to get a "yes" to the second option. If our working dynamic is that we are helping the client develop something, rather than doing it for them, acceptance will accrue on a day-by-day basis rather than as a handover or sign-off. Rather than a single sign-off, we should schedule staged reviews – and make it clear that if stakeholders change their minds, they will incur cost and time penalties. Expectations, as documented, should be met progressively rather than with a "big bang" deliverable. If we are going to introduce change or (especially in the case of data modeling) unfamiliar concepts, we need to take other stakeholders along with our thinking as it progresses, rather than presenting the accumulated result, and requiring them to accept it in one leap.

WRITING REPORTS

The tangible outcome of many assignments is a report. And the most common problem with reports is a focus on impressing rather than informing. Blame it on school! There, if we wanted good marks, our essays and assignments needed to demonstrate effort, originality, literary merit, and of course knowledge. In a business or technical report, these attributes become flaws. In particular, including material that the reader could be expected to know already, or which is not directly relevant to the assignment is likely to be seen as evidence of unnecessary effort and expense.

Re-check the expectations and write plainly and simply to address them. It can be helpful to start by writing a one page summary at the outset, as an aid to thinking about structure, then re-drafting it at the end. In any event, all reports should include such a summary, and, as with the rest of the report, stakeholders should have an opportunity to review and contribute as it develops.

FOLLOWING UP

On completion of a piece of work, it's easy to lose touch with the ongoing project. The model is complete and in the hands of the DBA; new challenges beckon; perhaps the project is one you'd rather not remember. Despite these temptations to do otherwise, you should make a practice of staying in touch with past clients. At the very least it shows that you had (and have) a commitment to the project rather than just the model – remember the importance of context!

There are other reasons for staying in touch in a formal, scheduled way, as well as for occasional informal catch-ups. Follow-up reviews provide an opportunity to correct errors and misunderstandings. Perhaps the data model needs modification (as distinct from "fudging"!) to cope with an overlooked requirement; or the definition of an entity is being misinterpreted. Ideally, a post-engagement review should be undertaken by your line manager with the key client, to provide feedback on your performance and input to your overall performance review.

By monitoring the way our work is used, we can assess its value in the context of the project or organization, and draw lessons for future work. Strategic work is seldom expected to provide immediate payoffs, but we have a professional duty to assure ourselves that it delivers the intended longer-term benefits. If it does, we have evidence that supports using the approach again. If not, we are bound to reconsider what we are recommending.

And remember, if things go wrong, blame often falls on those who have departed. By keeping in touch, you may avoid being included in that group.

CONTINUOUS IMPROVEMENT

Finally, a word on continuing to improve your ability to work effectively with others as a specialist and / or consultant. I suggest you develop the habit of observing your own interactions with experts and service providers from other fields – regular providers such as your physician, accountant, financial advisor, and travel agent, as well as one-off encounters. Look for what works and what doesn't: effective means of delivering advice, communicating, resolving problems, and less-effective approaches. Then, reflect on how you can adapt them to your own work.

EXERCISE 13: Keeping a Diary

Keep a diary for one month. Follow Graeme's lead, and at the end of every consulting day, write notes for yourself, including working hours, key events, and reflections. Include notes on any interactions with service providers where you were the client. Is there any behaviour that you can adapt – or avoid? Has this diary proven useful? Would you consider writing in your diary on an ongoing basis?

Key Points

- ✓ The biggest challenge for most data modelers is working with others: persuading business and technical people of the value of data modeling; getting access to business stakeholders and communicating effectively with them; building an effective working relationship with the database administration team.

- ✓ To improve your working relationships with others, *set expectations, stay on track*, and *achieve closure*.

- ✓ A successful data modeling engagement needs to be based on a set of expectations, understood and agreed by all stakeholders.

- ✓ Like other professionals, data modelers want to produce high-quality results – but need to remember that quality is *fitness for purpose* rather than an absolute standard.

- ✓ Asking questions such as "What does the final product look like?" can help clarify expectations.

SECTION V
Essential Topics Beyond Data Modeling

Section V introduces essential topics beyond data modeling. In Chapter 14, Bill Inmon explains unstructured data. Handling unstructured data is fast becoming part of our requirements, so we need to understand it better, as well as taxonomies and ontologies. In Chapter 15, Michael Blaha provides an overview of the Unified Modeling Language (UML). We conclude the book with Chapter 16, where I will address the top five most frequently asked questions in my classes.

Text, music, pictures
Turning my world upside down
Taxonomy, help!

By Bill Inmon

Bill Inmon has written 50 books, translated into 9 languages. He is considered to be the father of data warehousing. In this chapter, Bill explains unstructured data, along with taxonomies and ontologies.

UNSTRUCTURED DATA EXPLAINED

For years, the information technology community has focused on structured data. Structured data is data that is repetitive. There are many forms of structured data –

- bank activities
- insurance premium payments
- airline reservations
- order processing
- manufacturing job completion, and so forth.

In structured processing, the same activity is measured over and over. The only thing that changes from one activity to the next is the particulars of the activity. I go to my bank and cash a check. You go to your bank and cash a check. The only difference between my activity and yours is the date of the transaction, the amount of the transaction and the account that the transaction affected.

With structured data, the same type of activity repeats itself almost endlessly.

171

Indeed, even standard database management systems are optimized for storing structured data. One database record captures the information about one event and the next database record captures the particulars of the next event. Entire methodologies and disciplines have grown up around the processing of structured data. But there is another important kind of data that is not structured. There is textual or unstructured data. It is estimated that there is approximately four to five times as much unstructured data as there is structured data in the average corporation.

Textual or unstructured data fits no pattern and is not repetitive. As a simple example of unstructured data, consider email. When a person writes an email, there is no one editing it. The email can be short or long. The email can be in English, Spanish, or Swahili. The email may contain foul language. The text in the email may be in complete sentences or not. The word "thanks" may be abbreviated "thx". An individual who writes an email is free to write whatever he or she wants. There just aren't any rules for emails. Or reports. Or a thousand other forms of textual data.

Interestingly, some of the most important information in the corporation is in the form of text. There are literally thousands of forms of textual data that contain vital information for the corporation. And yet textual data is nowhere to be found in the corporate decision making process. Figure 14.1 shows that there are two very different kinds of data in the corporation – structured data and unstructured data.

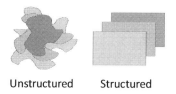

Unstructured   Structured

Figure 14.1 Two kinds of data in the corporation

The really good news is that there is now technology that can be used to read, integrate, and incorporate textual data into a standard relational database. In doing so, unstructured data can be incorporated into the corporate decision making process. The journey to incorporating unstructured data into corporate decisions begins with the abstraction of text.

DATA MODELING AND ABSTRACTION

The notion that systematization of data begins with abstraction comes from data modeling. For a long time now, system developers have used data modeling to get a grip on structured data. It is the data model and the abstraction behind the data model that allows large types of data to be compared, to be grouped, to be treated in a common fashion. Figure 14.2 shows that the data model becomes the link between structured data and the "real world".

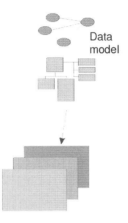

Figure 14.2 The data model is the link

The real world is usually the environment in which the system that is being modeled must operate. Typically, the real world consists of entities such as customers, products, payments, orders, transactions, shipments, and so forth. The real world is used as a basis for determining whether the data model that is based on an abstraction of the real world is "right" or "wrong". The more accurately the data model reflects the real world, the better.

The data model is useful for many purposes. It is useful for communications. It is useful for coordinating the development efforts of different groups of people over a lengthy period of time. It is useful for determining the overlap of information of different aspects of the real world. In short, the data model has many beneficial uses throughout the life of the systems that are being developed.

Modern system developers have learned that it is not advisable to build large and complex systems without a data model.

IMMUTABLE UNSTRUCTURED DATA

There is one underlying assumption that data modelers make about data models and the systems that are built beneath them. That assumption is that if there is a need to change the data model, the data model can be changed. Subsequently, the system that is to be built based on the data model can likewise be changed. In other words, if the government changes its mind about the length of the postal code, then the size and the format of the postal code can be increased in the data model and in the systems that are patterned after the data model. Most data modelers have taken this aspect of data modeling for granted. They simply assume that that is the way that data models and systems relate to each other. Figure 14.3 shows this aspect of the data model and the underlying systems.

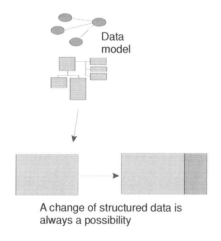

Data model

A change of structured data is always a possibility

Figure 14.3 Business changes lead to data model changes

When it comes to unstructured data, such an assumption is not realistic. Unlike data found in a structured system that is mutable, most text is not mutable. In other words, text cannot be changed once written. In most cases, this is just common sense. But in some cases, this aspect of the inability to change text fringes on illegality. For example, on a loan application, a bank is charged, by law, to capture whatever the applicant has written, even if what is written is known to be incorrect. As a simple example, a person supplies their birth date as occurring 5,000 years ago. The truth is that no one lives to be 5,000 years old (Methuselah notwithstanding). But the bank is obligated to capture what was written, even when what was written is known to be incorrect.

Once it has been written, most text cannot be changed. This feature of text is diametrically different from standard structured data found in a standard system.

TAXONOMIES EXPLAINED

The mechanism used to abstract information in text that is similar to a data model is a taxonomy. In its simplest form, a taxonomy is merely a list of related words. There are many, many forms of taxonomies in the real world. Some simple examples of taxonomies might be –

Cars
- Porsche
- Ford
- Volkswagen
- Honda
- Kia, and so forth

Or States
- Texas
- New Mexico
- Arizona
- Utah
- Colorado, and so forth

Or Games
- Football
- Hop scotch
- Tag
- Basketball
- Hockey, and so forth

In its simplest form, a taxonomy is merely a categorization of some words. Each word in the category has the same relationship to the category type as every other word. See Figure 14.4.

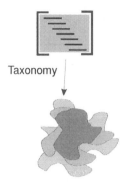

Taxonomy

Figure 14.4 A taxonomy can be used to classify the text found in unstructured data

As an example of how a taxonomy might be used, consider some simple raw text. The raw text looks like this:

"The young man loved to drive his Porsche. Whenever he passed a Ford, he felt a rush of adrenalin. But when he passed a Volkswagen, he felt sorry for the owner and considered it to be no special feat. Then one day he saw the new sporting model made by Honda. His insides churned."

When the reader addresses the text, the reader immediately understands the meaning of Porsche, Ford, Volkswagen, and Honda. But the computer attaches no special meaning to these words. However, when using a taxonomy against the raw text, the different occurrences of cars can be recognized. For example, by using the car taxonomy, the raw text can be transformed into:

"The young man loved to drive his Porsche/CAR. Whenever he passed a Ford/CAR, he felt a rush of adrenalin. But when he passed a Volkswagen/CAR, he felt sorry for the owner and considered it to be no special feat. Then one day he saw the new sporting model made by Honda/CAR. His insides churned."

PROCESSING RAW TEXT

By using a taxonomy, the raw text can be transformed into text that has values and categories recognizable to the computer. Using a taxonomy, the computer can now recognize what is and what is not a car. Now a query looking for all cars can be performed, and the search will find Fords, Porsches, Hondas, and so forth.

The value of the taxonomy applied to raw text is inestimable. One value is the ability to mitigate the effects of terminology. When any amount of text is gathered, it is almost inevitable that the text contains differences in terminology. For example, in medicine there are at least 20 ways to say "broken bone". Using a taxonomy, the different ways in which to say broken bone are synthesized into a common vocabulary. Once the taxonomy has been applied to raw text, the effects of terminology are mitigated.

And there are many more advantages of applying a taxonomy to raw text.

In many ways, a taxonomy is to text what a data model is to the data found in a structured system. Figure 14.5 shows this analogy.

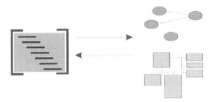

The taxonomy and the data model
are roughly equivalents

Figure 14.5 Taxonomies and data models are similar

See Figure 14.6.

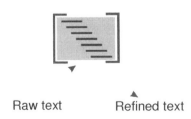

Raw text   Refined text

Figure 14.6 Taxonomy can produce refined text from raw text

There are many different ways to apply taxonomies to raw text. The simplest way to apply a taxonomy to raw text is to read a word of raw text and search all the words found in the taxonomy. Then, if there is a hit, apply the taxonomy classification to the raw text. Using the example that has been developed, the raw text contains the word "Porsche". The word "Porsche" is found in the taxonomy for "cars". Because a hit has occurred, the word "cars" is attached behind the word "Porsche". The result is text that looks like – "Porsche/cars". Once this attachment is made, the system can be queried looking for all references to "cars".

Note that there is a drawback to this approach. That drawback is performance. If there are n raw words to be processed and if there are m words in the taxonomy, then n x m comparisons must be made. Even at electronic speeds, this simple equation can become a stumbling block to efficient processing of raw text. This performance consideration is especially relevant in light of the fact that there is usually more than one taxonomy to be applied to raw text. For example when processing raw text there may be taxonomies for:

cars

gasoline stations

rest stops, and

auto repair shops.

Each word in each taxonomy is used in the processing of raw text. Therefore, when one considers the simple n x m equation, one must factor in ALL the words in ALL taxonomies when calculating m. See Figure 14.7.

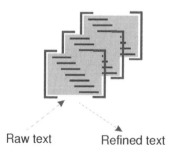

Raw text   Refined text

Figure 14.7 More than one taxonomy is applied to raw text in the normal case

There is another important consideration when applying a taxonomy to raw text. The taxonomy must be chosen according to its appropriateness to the raw text. To illustrate this factor consider the raw text:

"President Ford drove a Ford"

If the raw text that was being analyzed were about American presidents, then the analysis might look like:

"President Ford/38th president drove a Ford"

But if the raw text that was being analyzed pertained to automobiles, then the application of the taxonomy to the raw text might look like:

"President Ford drove a Ford/car"

In light of the appropriateness of a taxonomy to a body of raw text, consider the following. Suppose the raw text being analyzed related to salt water fishing. Some of the taxonomies that apply might be:

> types of fish
>
> fishing methods
>
> oceans of the world
>
> deep sea oil platforms.

But it is very unlikely that the following taxonomies would be applied to the text for deep sea fishing:

> Sarbanes Oxley classifications of data
>
> National Football league teams
>
> Top 100 professional golfers
>
> Farming methods in the Ohio River valley.

CAPTURING TAXONOMY PROPERTIES

Taxonomies themselves have some interesting properties. One interesting property is that of the number of words in the taxonomy. A taxonomy can contain only a few selected words or it can contain lots of words. In addition, the relationship of the taxonomy to the classification of the taxonomy may vary slightly from word to word. As an example, consider the taxonomy:

Car

- Porsche
- Ford
- Volkswagen
- Honda
- Humvee
- Jeep

While it is true that each of the vehicle types listed are indeed cars (or at least vehicles), there is nevertheless a difference between cars. A Porsche is normally thought of as a sports car. A Ford is normally thought of as a family car. A Jeep is thought of as an off road vehicle.

But there are other differences. A Honda is thought of as a Japanese car. A Volkswagen is thought of as a German car. A Ford is thought of as an American car.

A taxonomy, then, is a classification of just one aspect of the objects being classified together.

Another property of a taxonomy is the fact that different levels of classification may exist within a taxonomy. For example, consider the following taxonomy:

Car
    Sports car
- Porsche
- Ferrari

    Off Road
- Jeep
- Humvee
- Mitsubishi

    Family
- Honda
- Ford
- Chrysler

It is entirely possible to have different levels of classifications or different levels of classifications within different levels of classifications. In fact, there can be all sorts of classifications within classifications. This leads naturally to the fact that it is entirely possible to have recursive relationships within a taxonomy. As an example of a recursive relationship within a taxonomy consider the following taxonomy –

Car
   Sports car
      o Porsche
      o Ferrari
   Off Road
      o Jeep
      o Humvee
      o Mitsubishi
      o Porsche
   Family
      o Honda
      o Ford
      o Chrysler

In this taxonomy, Porsche appears twice. Porsche appears as a sports car because of its world famous 911 series. But Porsche also appears in the off road classification because of its Cayenne product. See Figure 14.8.

Data within the taxonomy
can be recursive

Figure 14.8 Recursive relationships can appear within classifications themselves

Recursive relationships are interesting unto themselves. When a recursive relationship appears, interesting things can happen. Care must be taken because they require special programming attention. For one thing, programmers have to be careful because it is very easy to fall into the trap of very complex coding (that is almost impossible to debug), or loops that repeat themselves endlessly (infinite loops).

MAINTAINING TAXONOMIES OVER TIME

Another issue that occurs with taxonomies is that they must be maintained over time. As the world changes, taxonomies must also change. For example, in 1945, would Honda have been included in a list of cars? The answer is no. In 1990, would George W. Bush have been included in a list of presidents? The answer is no. In 1950, would Kazakhstan been included in a list of countries? The answer is no. As the world changes, so change the taxonomies. This means that periodically, taxonomies need to be maintained. See Figure 14.9.

The fact that taxonomies periodically need to be maintained brings to the surface an interesting question - suppose raw text has been refined by being passed against a taxonomy. Then one day, the taxonomy is updated. Does this mean that all text that has been refined must now be reprocessed against the updated taxonomy? Or is it sufficient to merely process all future raw text against the updated taxonomy?

The answer is that on a case by case basis, raw text can be refined or not. There is no generic right or wrong here. Stated differently, some raw text will, indeed, need to be reprocessed when the taxonomy in maintained, while other raw text will not need to be reprocessed when the taxonomy is updated.

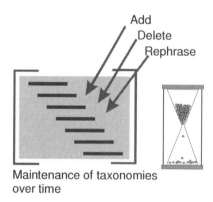

Add
Delete
Rephrase

Maintenance of taxonomies
over time

Figure 14.9 The need for periodically maintaining taxonomies

It is easy to see how simple taxonomies can be built and can be used. What may not be obvious is that taxonomies may consist of not only words, but phrases as well. For example, there may be a taxonomy of phrases that looks like Famous Hollywood lines:

go ahead, make my day (Clint Eastwood as Dirty Harry)

frankly my dear, I don't give a damn (Clark Gable in Gone With The Wind)

who are those guys (Paul Newman in Butch Cassidy And The Sundance Kid)

you couldn't handle the truth (Jack Nicholson in A Few Good Men)

this corn is special (Ned Beatty in Deliverance).

See Figure 14.10.

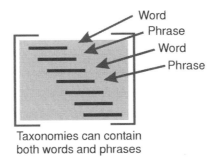

Taxonomies can contain
both words and phrases

Figure 14.10 Both words and phrases can be found in a taxonomy

TRACING TAXONOMIES

So where do taxonomies come from? Taxonomies come from categorizations of words found in the real world based on real world relationships. The real world may be the world of business, healthcare, recreation, humor, religion, politics, family history, etc. There simply is no limitation as to where taxonomies can be found.

In some cases, the taxonomies are captured formally, and in other cases, they are captured informally. In some cases, there is a desire to create an exhaustive list of all the words and phrases in a category. In other cases, there is only a need for the creation of a representative list of words found in a category.

ONTOLOGIES EXPLAINED

There are many different forms of taxonomies. Related to a taxonomy is the ontology. In many regards, an ontology is a superset of a taxonomy. An ontology is a taxonomy in which there are relationships between the different words found in the ontology. See Figure 14.11.

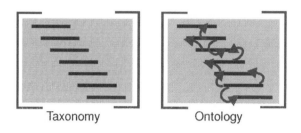

Taxonomy   Ontology

Figure 14.11 A taxonomy and an ontology

One of the interesting features of a taxonomy is that the taxonomy can cross languages. For example, a taxonomy in English can be translated to the same taxonomy in Spanish and lose none of the meaning of the taxonomy. While this may appear as a novel feature of taxonomies, it oftentimes has very real application. For example, suppose that an organization has customers who speak Spanish and other customers who speak English. The text can be collected in both languages. The Spanish version of the taxonomy can then be used to categorize the words in Spanish. The words in Spanish can be translated using the parallel categorization in English. In such a manner, a single language categorization can be created where the raw text is found in more than one language.

EXERCISE 14: LOOKING FOR A TAXONOMY

Identify at least one taxonomy in use within your organization. Would you consider this taxonomy to be well-defined and fully leveraged in your organization? Why or why not?

Key Points

✓ There are two basic forms of data – structured data and unstructured data. In order to create an abstraction of structured data, data models are created. But textual data differs fundamentally from structured data in that unstructured data cannot be changed, while structured data can usually be changed.

✓ In order to create an abstraction of unstructured data, taxonomies are used. The taxonomies are useful for organizing unstructured data into common categories.

✓ Taxonomies, then, are to unstructured data what data models are to structured data.

✓ Taxonomies are the basis under which text is abstracted. The abstraction of text is valuable because of the ability to overcome different terminology in text, to use query languages to find classes of data, and to organize text according to the general context of the unstructured data.

✓ An ontology is a taxonomy in which there are relationships between the different words found in the ontology.

CHAPTER 15
What is UML?

Capture the business
Data, process – tightly linked
Enter UML

By Michael Blaha

For the past 15 years, Michael Blaha has been a consultant and trainer in conceiving, architecting, modeling, and designing databases. He also has extensive experience in database reverse engineering for product assessment and business due diligence. He has authored six US patents, five books, and many papers. Blaha received his D.Sc. degree from Washington University in St. Louis and is an alumnus of the GE Global Research Center in Schenectady, NY. His latest book is *Patterns of Data Modeling*. In this chapter, Michael discusses the Unified Modeling Language (UML) from the perspective of database applications. He will cover the diagrams of the UML that are most pertinent to database applications. Note that in this chapter, the term 'model' refers to UML models, not data models.

UML EXPLAINED

A UML *model* is an abstraction of an application that lets you thoroughly understand it. Models are used for programming, creating databases, and other purposes—although we emphasize databases here. A model provides a roadmap for an application, similar to a blueprint for a building that is studied and revised many times before it is built. There are many reasons for building software via models:

- **Better quality**. Your application can be no better than the underlying thought. ACM Turing award winner Fred Brooks contends "that conceptual integrity is the most important consideration in system design." [Brooks-1995]

- **Reduced cost**. You can shift your activities towards the relatively inexpensive front end of software development and away from costly debugging and maintenance.

- **Faster time to market**. It is faster to deal with difficulties at the conceptual stage than to deal with them when software has been cast into programming and database code.

- **Better performance**. A sound model simplifies database tuning.

- **Improved communication**. Models reduce misunderstandings and promote consensus between developers, customers, and other stakeholders.

Models are helpful for software that is purchased, as well as software that is developed. You need to understand your requirements and their manifestation in software before you can assess the strengths and weaknesses of various vendor products.

The UML (Unified Modeling Language) is a graphical language for modeling software development artifacts. It spans the range of the lifecycle, from conceptualization to analysis, then design, and ultimately, implementation.

The UML arose from the many object-oriented (OO) approaches to software development that were prevalent in the 1990s. OO approaches had become popular, but the incompatible notations and terminologies were fracturing the software community and causing confusion. In reality, there was little substantive difference between the various approaches. The purpose of the UML was to rise above this babble and standardize concepts and notation so that developers could read each other's models and build on each other's efforts. One benefit of the UML is that a single notation can address both programming and database concerns and bridge the cultural gap across the two communities. Another more subtle benefit is that operations provide a hook for attaching database functionality — stored procedures, referential integrity, triggers, and views.

The UML has been developed under the auspices of the OMG (Object Management Group) [www.omg.org]. The initial formulation was driven by Grady Booch, James Rumbaugh, and Ivar Jacobson, but over the years, there have been dozens of significant contributors. The current release is UML 2.0.

Note that the UML standardizes concepts and notation. The UML does not address the issue of software development process. There are a number of processes in the literature for how to use UML notation to develop software.

The UML has a variety of diagrams, including the following:

- **Class diagram**. Involves classes, relationships, and generalizations. Specifies data structure.

- **Object diagram**. Concerns individual objects and links among objects. Shows examples of data structure.

- **Use case diagram**. Specifies the high-level functionality of software from the perspective of an end-user. Also notes the external actors involved with the software.

- **State diagram**. Concerns states and events that cause transitions between states. Describes the discrete, temporal behavior of objects.

- **Activity diagram**. Shows the workflow for an individual piece of functionality.

- **Sequence diagram**. Shows how processes interact, with whom and what, and in what order.

The UML has been warmly embraced by programmers and is often used during the development of programming code.

However, the UML has had a mixed reception by the database community. Many database practitioners are aware of the UML, but do not use it. The problem is that the UML standardization process ignored the database community. UML jargon emphasizes programming, which puts off many database developers. The irony is that the programming jargon is superficial and in reality, the UML has much to offer for database application development, as this chapter will show.

A strength of the UML is its large variety of diagrams. For general software development, it is likely that the UML will have all the diagrams that you need. For specialized problems, the UML may be lacking and you may need to include additional kinds of diagrams.

A weakness of the UML is its large variety of diagrams. However, do keep in mind that you don't have to use all of the UML models. Just use the ones that are helpful for your applications. We often construct class models. On occasion, we also prepare use cases, state diagrams, activity diagrams, and sequence diagrams.

MODELING INPUTS

It is important to consider all inputs when modeling software. In particular, you should be expansive in your search for information and not obsess with use cases. Use cases are significant, but are only one information source. A skilled developer should be adaptable and able to glean requirements from all available resources. Sources of requirements include the following:

- **Use cases**. Many business persons think naturally in terms of use cases and find them convenient for specifying requirements.

- **Business documentation**. Business justification, screen mock-ups, sample reports, and other documentation are often already prepared and available for the asking.

- **User interviews**. Developers can question business experts for missing information and clarification.

- **Technical reviews**. Technologists and line managers can also contribute to the content of a model. For example, they may have prior application or business experience.

- **Related applications**. Consider systems that are to be replaced, as well as systems that will remain, but overlap the new system.

- **Standard models**. Some types of applications have models that are available from standards organizations. For example, the OMG has published the *common warehouse metamodel* to standardize data exchange for data warehouses. [Poole-2002]

MODELING OUTPUTS

Modeling outputs include diagrams, of course, but diagrams alone are insufficient. When we prepare models for applications, we often deliver the following outputs:

- **Diagrams**. Diagrams apply rigor to requirements so that they can be thoroughly considered and acted upon.

- **Explanation**. Sometimes we write a narrative that interleaves diagrams with explanation. On other occasions, especially if our model is delivered via the files of a modeling tool, we prepare a data dictionary and attach definitions to major model elements.

- **Database structure**. You can convert a model into a database schema by applying straightforward rules as [Blaha-2005] explains.

- **Converted data**. Often, there is data from a prior application or related applications that can seed the database for a new application. For example, you may have a customer list to seed a new marketing application.

CLASS MODEL EXPLAINED

The UML *class model* describes data structure — the classes that are involved and how they relate to one another. The major concepts in the class model are classes, associations, and generalizations. Figure 15.1 shows a sample class model. We will first explain the meaning of the model, and then explain the UML constructs. You'll notice that the class model looks a lot like a data model.

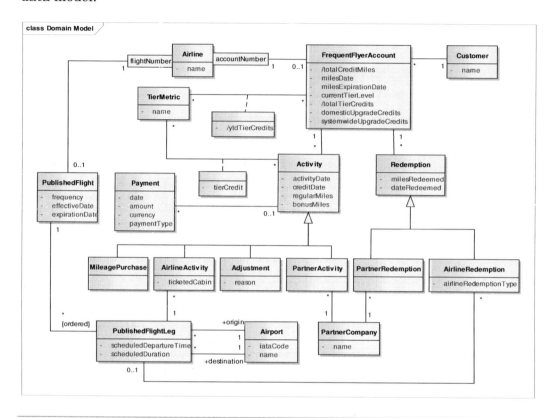

Figure 15.1 Sample class model

In Figure 15.1, a customer can have multiple frequent flyer accounts, though normally a customer has only a single account for an airline. Each frequent flyer account has a unique account number for a given issuing airline.

Each account has a total number of credit miles that can be computed from the underlying activities and redemptions. There is a date as of which the total credit miles are computed, as well as a date that the miles expire. Airline practice is to extend the expiration date as long as there are sufficient activities and redemptions. An account may have upgrade credits to first class for domestic travel. An account may also have system-wide upgrade credits for traveling overseas. A frequent flyer account is a holder for activities that earn miles as well as redemptions that consume miles.

There are various kinds of activities. A mileage purchase is the procurement of credit miles in exchange for payment. Airline activity is the nominal purpose of frequent flyer accounts — in return for airline travel, a customer receives mileage credits. The credits vary according to the ticketed cabin as well as promotional rules that vary over time. The logic for awarding credit is outside the scope of the model. An adjustment corrects an error or posts credit due to unusual circumstances (such as compensation to a customer after a troublesome flight). Partner activity is also important for frequent flyer accounts. Airlines market the accounts to their partners — such as car rental companies, hotels, and credit card companies — who attract customers by paying the airlines for mileage credit.

Similarly, there are various kinds of redemptions. Many redemptions are for free airline flights or to upgrade the cabin from the ticketed fare. Other redemptions are via partners, such as free car rentals and free merchandise.

Airlines offer published flights that have a frequency (such as every day except Saturday). Published flights have effective and expiration dates. A published flight consists of flight legs; each flight leg has an origin airport and a destination airport. The distinction between flights and flight legs is important when dealing with flights. It is airline practice to have some flight numbers that start from a city, stop in an intermediate city, and then arrive in a destination city. The whole sequence has the same flight number and customers can purchase the full flight or any of the constituent legs.

Each account has a current tier level. For example, the tier levels for American Airlines are gold, platinum, and executive platinum. Customers with higher tier levels receive more perks and flying benefits. The accumulated tier credits from account activity determines the customer's tier level. There can be different ways of computing the tier level (tier metric) — American Airlines uses points, miles, and segments (count of traveled flight legs).

CLASS

An *object* is a concept, abstraction, or thing with identity that has meaning for an application. A *class* describes a group of objects with the same attributes, operations, kinds of relationships, and semantic intent. The UML symbol for a class is a box with the name of the class in the top portion of the box. In Figure 15.1, Airline, FrequentFlyerAccount, and Activity are examples of classes. A class is similar to an entity in a data model, but it is broader in that it includes operations.

The second portion of a class box shows the attribute names for the class. An *attribute* is a named property of a class that describes a value held by each object of the class. In Figure 15.1, FrequentFlyerAccount has seven attributes, Airline has one attribute, and MileagePurchase has zero attributes.

Several of the attribute names in Figure 15.1 are prefaced with a slash (/) symbol. The slash is UML notation for derived data. For example, **totalCreditMiles** is computed (derived) from the posted activities and redemptions. Although Figure 15.1 does not show it, each attribute can have a multiplicity that specifies the number of possible values for instantiation. The most common options are a mandatory single value [1], an optional single value [0..1], and many [*]. Multiplicity specifies whether an attribute is mandatory or optional (whether an attribute can be null). Multiplicity also indicates if an attribute is single valued or can be a collection of values.

The third portion of a class box (not shown in Figure 15.1) shows the operations for a class. An *operation* is a function or procedure that may be applied to or by objects in a class. Operations are used frequently when using UML class diagrams for programming. Sometimes they are also used for database design, such as when an operation is written as a database stored procedure. For example, a stored procedure could update the **totalCreditMiles** for a **FrequentFlyerAccount** each time there is an **Activity** or **Redemption**. There might be another stored procedure that checks a **FrequentFlyerAccount** for sufficient credit miles to cover a **Redemption**.

ASSOCIATION

A *link* is a physical or conceptual connection among objects. An *association* is a description of a group of links with common structure and semantics. The links of an association connect objects from the same classes. An association describes a set of potential links in the same way that a class describes a set of potential objects. The UML notation for an association is a line (possibly with multiple line segments) between classes. In Figure 15.1 the line between **PublishedFlight** and **PublishedFlightLeg** is an association. Similarly, there are two lines and two associations between **PublishedFlightLeg** and **Airport**. An association is similar to a relationship on a data model.

A binary association has two ends. (The UML supports ternary and higher order associations, even though they seldom occur.) Each end can have a name and multiplicity. *Multiplicity* specifies the number of instances of one class that may relate to a single instance of an associated class. The UML specifies multiplicity with an interval. The most common multiplicities are "1", "0..1", and "*" (the special symbol for "many"). In Figure 15.1, there is one origin Airport and one destination **Airport** for a **PublishedFlightLeg**. (Origin and destination are association end names.) An **Airport** can have many **PublishedFlightLegs** having it as an origin, as well as many **PublishedFlightLegs** having it as a destination.

Usually the objects on a "many" association end have no explicit order, and you can regard them as a set. Sometimes, however, the objects do have an explicit order. You can indicate an ordered set of objects by writing "{ordered}" next to the appropriate association end. In Figure 15.1, the **PublishedFlightLegs** for a **PublishedFlight** are ordered. For example, a through flight could first go from St. Louis to Chicago and then from Chicago to Buffalo.

An *association class* is an association that is also a class. Like the links of an association, the instances of an association class derive identity from instances of the component classes. Like a class, an association class can have attributes and operations and participate in associations. The UML notation for an association class is a box that is connected to the corresponding association with a dotted line. Figure 15.1 has two association classes, one between **FrequentFlyerAccount** and **TierMetric** and the other between **TierMetric** and **Activity**. These two association classes each have one attribute. An association class is similar to an associative entity that resolves a many-to-many relationship.

A *qualified association* is an association in which an attribute called the *qualifier* partially or fully disambiguates the objects for a "many" association end. The qualifier selects among the target objects, reducing the effective multiplicity, often from "many" to "one". Names are often qualifiers. The notation for a qualifier is a small box on the end of the association line near the source class. The source class plus the qualifier yields the target class. Figure 15.1 has two qualified associations. The **accountNumber** for a **FrequentFlyerAccount** is unique within the context of the issuing **Airline**. Similarly, the **flightNumber** for a **PublishedFlight** is unique within the context of an **Airline**. In data modeling terms, the **Airline** primary key + **accountNumber** is a unique key for **FrequentFlyerAccount**, and the **Airline** primary key + **flightNumber** is a unique key for **PublishedFlight**.

Aggregation is a strong form of association in which an aggregate object is made of component parts. The most significant property of aggregation is transitivity (if A is part of B and B is part of C, then A is part of C) and anti symmetry (if A is part of B, then B is not part of A). Figure 15.1 does not show any aggregations.

Composition is a form of aggregation with two additional constraints. A constituent part can belong to at most one assembly. Figure 15.1 does not show composition.

GENERALIZATION

Generalization is the relationship between a class (the *superclass*) and one or more variations of the class (the *subclasses*). Generalization organizes classes by their similarities and differences, structuring the description of objects. The superclass holds common attributes, operations, and associations; the subclasses add specific attributes, operations, and associations. Each subclass *inherits* the attributes, operations, and associations of its superclass. A hollow arrowhead denotes generalization and points to the superclass. You should be familiar with similar concepts in data modeling – subtyping, supertypes, and subtypes.

Figure 15.1 has two generalizations. One generalization has a superclass of **Activity** and subclasses of **MileagePurchase**, **AirlineActivity**, **Adjustment**, and **PartnerActivity**. The other generalization has a superclass of **Redemption** and subclasses of **PartnerRedemption** and **AirlineRedemption**.

USE CASE MODEL EXPLAINED

The UML *use case model* describes functionality in terms of actors and real-world behavior (use cases) that they perform. The focus is on how the software interacts with outside actors.

ACTOR

An *actor* is a direct external user of a system. Actors include humans, external devices, and other software systems. A class can be bound to multiple actors if it has different facets to its behavior. The UML symbol for an actor is a stick figure with the name of the actor as a legend below the figure. Figure 15.2 has several examples of actors and also shows actor generalization (an **Agent** may be a **ComputerAgent** or a **HumanAgent**). Figure 15.3 shows three of the actors from Figure 15.2.

USE CASE

A *use case* is a coherent piece of functionality that a system can provide by interacting with actors. Use cases emphasize externally-perceived functionality rather than the details of implementation. The UML symbol for a use case is an oval with the name of the use case inside. A use case is connected to pertinent actors via solid lines. Figure 15.2 shows actors for the frequent flyer example.

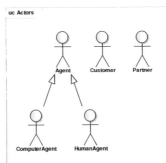

Figure 15.2 Actors for the frequent flyer example

- **Agent**. Agents participate in use cases such as opening and closing an account. We distinguish between human agents and computer agents because they may differ in their precise functionality. The distinction could be important to an airline's business.

- **Customer**. Customer is an obvious actor. The entire purpose of the frequent flyer software is to respond to customers.

- **Partner**. Partner companies are also external entities that interact with the frequent flyer software.

We considered making airline an actor, but it seems that airline functionality occurs via agents that are affiliated with an airline. We should revisit that decision as we add use cases. There may be additional actors that Figure 15.2 does not show. You can find actors by thinking through usage scenarios (use cases) and paying attention to high-level external entities that interact with the software. Figure 15.3 shows six use cases for the frequent flyer example.

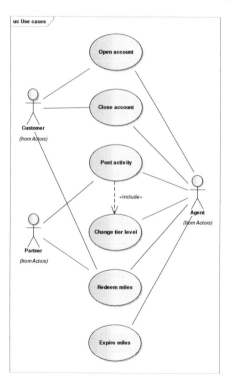

Figure 15.3 Sample use cases

- **Open account**. Create a new frequent flyer account for a customer. Try to ensure that the customer does not already have a frequent flyer account. Set the total credit miles and total tier credits to zero. Post an adjustment if there is a promotional reward for opening a new account.

- **Close account**. Set a date that flags a frequent flyer account as no longer active. (Need to add this to the class model.) After some further passage of time, destroy the frequent flyer account and any associated activity and redemption. This two-phase approach could be helpful if there is a mistake or a change of heart by a customer.

- **Post activity**. Process new activity for a frequent flyer account and add it to the database. Update the total credit miles, miles date, mileage expiration date, and the total tier credits. If there are sufficient tier credits via one of the metrics, invoke the change tier level use case. (Or alternatively, scan all the accounts and change the tier level as appropriate.)

- **Change tier level**. Raise the tier level upon sufficient activity according to a tier metric. Lower the tier level when there has been insufficient activity to maintain a tier level for the past reporting period (a calendar year at American Airlines).

- **Redeem miles**. Give the customer the requested reward and debit his/her frequent flyer account. Ensure that the account has sufficient miles to cover the requested reward.

- **Expire miles**. Post an adjustment to zero the total credit miles if the account has not had activity within a specified time interval. (The time interval is a business policy. The current policy for American Airlines is that an account must have activity every 18 months or the total is zeroed.)

Note that the use cases have different combinations of actors. All the use cases interact with **Agent**. Only two use cases interact with **Partner** and three interact with **Customer**.

The *Post activity* use case includes the *Change tier level* use case, as the posting of an activity can cause a change of tier level. The *includes* is an example of a use case relationship and is shown with an arrow and an annotated dotted line.

EXERCISE 15: CREATING A USE CASE

Find an opportunity to build a use case. Did you find the use case to be essential in developing the requirements deliverable?

Key Points

- ✓ A UML model is an abstraction of an application that lets you thoroughly understand it. The most significant UML models for databases are the class model and the use case model.

- ✓ The UML class model describes data structure — the classes that are involved and how they relate to one another. The major concepts in the class model are classes, associations, and generalizations.

- ✓ An object is a concept, abstraction, or thing with identity that has meaning for an application. A class describes a group of objects with the same attributes, operations, kinds of relationships, and semantic intent. An attribute is a named property of a class that describes a value held by each object of the class. An operation is a function or procedure that may be applied to or by objects in a class.

- ✓ A link is a physical or conceptual connection among objects. An association is a description of a group of links with common structure and semantics.

- ✓ The UML use case model describes functionality in terms of actors and real-world behavior (use cases) that they perform. An actor is a direct external user of a system.

REFERENCES

[Blaha-2005] Michael Blaha and James Rumbaugh. *Object-Oriented Modeling and Design with UML, 2nd Edition*. Upper Saddle River, NJ: Prentice Hall, 2005.

[Brooks-1995] Frederick P. Brooks, Jr. *The Mythical Man-Month, Anniversary Edition*. Boston, MA: Addison-Wesley, 1995.

[Chen-1976] PPS Chen. The Entity-Relationship model—Toward a Unified View of Data. *ACM Transactions on Database Systems 1*, 1 (March 1976).

[Poole-2002] John Poole, Dan Chang, Douglas Tolbert, and David Mellor. *Common Warehouse Metamodel*. New York: OMG Press, 2002.

[Rumbaugh-2005] James Rumbaugh, Ivar Jacobson, and Grady Booch. *The Unified Modeling Language Reference Manual, Second Edition*. Boston, MA: Addison-Wesley, 2005.

CHAPTER 16
What are the Top 5 most frequently asked modeling questions?

Many industries
Yet similar challenges
Learn once, use often

This chapter contains the top five questions that have been asked over the last few years during data modeling training. If you have a question that is not listed here, feel free to email it to me at me@stevehoberman.com.

1. WHAT IS METADATA?

When most IT people are asked for their definition of metadata, before we can even think about what it really means, we hear ourselves say out loud, "Data about data." This is, however, a poor definition. As we know from our discussion of definitions in Chapter 12 on the Data Model Scorecard, a good definition is clear, complete, and correct. Although the "Data about data" definition is correct, it is not clear or complete. It is not clear, since businesspeople need to understand what metadata means and I have never found someone who responds with "Ah, I get it now" after hearing the "data about data" explanation. It is not a complete definition because it does not provide examples nor distinguish how metadata really differs from data. So we need a better definition for the term metadata.

I spoke on a metadata-related topic with several DAMA chapters and user groups. Collectively, we came up with the following definition for metadata:

Metadata is text, voice, or image that describes what the audience wants or needs to see or experience. The audience could be a person, group, or software program. Metadata is important because it aids in clarifying and finding the actual data.

A particular context or usage can turn what we traditionally consider data into metadata. For example, search engines allow users to enter keywords to retrieve web pages. These keywords are traditionally data, but in the context of search engines they play the role of metadata. Much the same way that a particular person can be an Employee in one role and a Customer in another role, text, voice or image can play different roles - sometimes playing 'data' and sometimes playing 'metadata', depending on what is important to a particular subject or activity.

There are at least six types of metadata: business (also known as 'semantic'), storage, process, display, project, and program.

Examples of business metadata are definitions, tags, and business names. Examples of storage metadata are database column names, formats, and volumetrics. Examples of process metadata are source/target mappings, data load metrics, and transformation logic. Examples of display metadata are display format, screen colors, and screen type (i.e. tablet vs laptop). Examples of project metadata are functional requirements, project plans, and weekly status reports. Examples of program metadata are the Zachman Framework, DAMA-DMBOK, and naming standards documentation.

2. HOW DO YOU QUANTIFY THE VALUE OF THE LOGICAL DATA MODEL?

The logical data model captures how the business works independent of technology. This view must be understood and agreed on before any development can take place. Skipping the logical data model leads to assumptions on how the business works and what they need from an application. When a new house is built, the architect uses a blueprint as a communication medium with the homeowners. The blueprint is the business solution to the home, in the same way as the data model is the business solution to an application. If a house is built without a blueprint, many assumptions will be made during construction, and there is a very good chance the customer (homeowner) will not be satisfied with the results.

It can be challenging to put a financial value or other quantifiable measure on the value of a particular logical data model, for the same reason it can be challenging to put a financial value on a particular blueprint. How much is a robust database design or accurate blueprint worth? Instead of quantifying the value of a logical data model, we can quantify the *cost* of not having a logical data model through symptoms such as poor data quality. Find stories on the internet or front page of the newspaper illustrating what happens when there is poor information available. Get good at telling these stories and make sure to include the figures on how much these companies lost because of a data quality issue, or how much could have been saved in terms of money or credibility if the data was of high quality.

For example, Ben Ettlinger, a lead data administrator, is a friend of mine who illustrates the importance of data quality, and therefore the data model, with a story about how NASA lost a $125 million Mars orbiter because one engineering team used metric units while another used English units for a key spacecraft operation. The logical data model can eliminate or minimize data quality issues such as this.

3. WHERE DOES XML FIT?

Extensible Markup Language (XML) is a type of data model which displays information in a hierarchy format using human-readable tags, allowing both people and software applications to more easily exchange and share information. XML is both useful and powerful for the same reasons any data model is useful and powerful: it is easy to understand, can be technology-independent, and enables representing complex problems with simple syntax. Similar to distinguishing conceptual data models from logical data models from physical data models, XML distinguishes the data content from formatting (e.g. blue, Arial, 15 point font) from rules. XML rules are represented through a schema, such as a Document Type Definition (DTD) or XML Schema Document (XSD). The schema specifies the rules for the data in an XML document in much the same way as a data model specifies the rules for the data in a database structure. The XML data content is displayed in the form of an XML document and is equivalent to one or more entity instances on a data model.

Figure 16.1 contains an XML document based on an example from Wikipedia.

```
<recipe name="bread" prep_time="5 mins" cook_time="3 hours">

  <title>Basic bread</title>

  <ingredient amount="8" unit="cup">Flour</ingredient>
```

```
<ingredient amount="10" unit="grams">Yeast</ingredient>

<ingredient amount="4" unit="cup" state="warm">Water</ingredient>

<ingredient amount="1" unit="teaspoon">Salt</ingredient>

<instructions>

  <step>Mix all ingredients together.</step>

  <step>Knead thoroughly.</step>

  <step>Cover with a cloth, and leave for one hour.</step>

  <step>Knead again.</step>

  <step>Place in a bread baking tin.</step>

  <step>Cover with a cloth, and leave for one hour.</step>

  <step>Bake at 180 degrees Celsius for 30 minutes.</step>

  </instructions>

</recipe>
```

Figure 16.1 Recipe XML document

The terms such as '<step>' are called 'tags'. The data within each pair of tags is called a 'value'. So the value for the tag pair <title> and </title> is 'Basic bread'.

Along with the schema for this XML document, we can learn quite a bit about the actual data. For example, we know that a **Recipe** may contain **Ingredients** and **Instructions** may contain **Steps**. Because XML is hierarchy-based, however, the rules only go one way. That is, we know a **Recipe** may contain **Ingredients**, but can an **Ingredient** belong to more than one **Recipe**? I email out monthly Design Challenges (add your email address at www.stevehoberman.com), and in a recent Design Challenge Norman Daoust, business analysis consultant and trainer, summarized this: "XML documents frequently only indicate the cardinality of relationships on one end of the relationship, not both ends."

Therefore, we can take this XML document and schema, and by asking additional business questions, derive a logical data model such as that in Figure 16.2. Sample values are shown in Table 16.1.

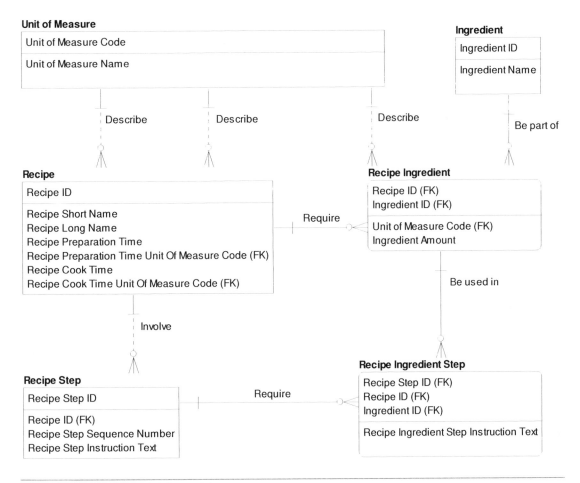

Figure 16.2 Recipe logical data model

Recipe

Recipe Id	Recipe Short Name	Recipe Long Name	Recipe Preparation Time	Recipe Preparation Time Unit Of Measure Code	Recipe Cook Time	Recipe Cook Time Unit Of Measure Code
123	bread	Basic bread	5	01	3	02

Unit Of Measure

Unit Of Measure Code	Unit Of Measure Name
01	Minute
02	Hour
03	Cup
04	Gram
05	Teaspoon

Ingredient

Ingredient Id	Ingredient Name
1	Flour
2	Yeast
3	Water
4	Salt

Recipe Ingredient

Recipe Id	Ingredient Id	Unit Of Measure Code	Ingredient Amount
123	1	03	8
123	2	04	10
123	3	03	4
123	4	05	1

Recipe Step

Recipe Step Id	Recipe Id	Recipe Step Sequence Number	Recipe Step Instruction Text
45	123	1	Mix all ingredients together.
46	123	2	Knead thoroughly.
47	123	3	Cover with a cloth, and leave for one hour.
48	123	4	Knead again.
49	123	5	Place in a bread baking tin.
50	123	6	Cover with a cloth, and leave for one hour.
51	123	7	Bake at 180 degrees Celsius for 30 minutes.

Recipe Ingredient Step

Recipe Step Id	Recipe Id	Ingredient Id	Recipe Ingredient Step Instruction Text
45	123	1	
45	123	2	
45	123	3	
45	123	4	

Table 16.1 Recipe logical data model values

Take note all of the business questions that would need to be added to arrive at this model, a small sample being:

- Can the **Recipe** have more than one long name (i.e. title)?
- Is **Recipe Short Name** really the natural key for **Recipe**?
- Is **Ingredient Name** really the natural key for **Ingredient**?
- Can an **Ingredient** belong to more than one **Recipe**?
- Can a **Recipe Step** require more than one **Recipe Ingredient**?

XML is in widespread use in our industry. The analyst and modeler can leverage XML to better understand a business area and build a more accurate data model. This is especially true in modeling industry standards. There are many industries that formalized on XML standards so that they can exchange information. One example is ePub, an XML standard for exchanging publishing information across organizations within the publishing industry. Leveraging these standards can make it possible to build more accurate enterprise data models and more useful applications that use industry-wide terminology and rules.

4. WHERE DOES AGILE FIT?

Agile means 'quick' and 'adept'. When applied to application development, agile translates into rapid delivery of high-quality software. Agile usually means there are many project-focused iterations until the project is complete. Proponents of agile say the project-focused approach produces high quality results in much less time than a typical software development methodology. Opponents of agile say the focus of agile is on the project at the expense of the program, meaning usually the enterprise perspective and 'big picture' are not given the attention they require. This is not a book on agile pros and cons, so I will stop with this discussion.

There are really two questions here: "Where are data models in an agile environment?" and "Where should data modeling take place in an agile environment?"

The answer to the first question is that usually data models are non-existent or of poor quality in an agile environment. I have taught classes onsite for many organizations using an agile approach and have consistently witnessed few data models been built. The reason is that agile focuses more on process and prototypes than data snapshots and building data models takes valuable time away from software development.

The answer to the second question, "Where should data modeling take place in an agile environment?" is the same as for any other project. Data modeling should be a process to find out what the business wants and to document these requirements consistent with other organization data models and views. Data modeling requires asking lots of questions – regardless of the software methodology chosen, these questions still need to be asked.

5. HOW DO I KEEP MY MODELING SKILLS SHARP?

Look for every opportunity to model or participate in the analysis and modeling process, even outside the traditional roles of a data modeler. The more roles we play around the modeling space, the greater our modeling skills become. For example, after modeling for a number of years, I decided to try development. As a developer, I became one of the customers of the data model, looking at the model with a different eye from that of the modeler. I became able to anticipate questions such as these in my design:

- How can I efficiently populate this structure with an extract, transform, and load (ETL) tool?
- Are there minor modifications I can make to the data model to make the development less complex and take less time?
- How can we extract data out as rapidly as possible for reporting?

Thinking of these questions during my modeling helped me become a more pragmatic data modeler. It broadened my view on the physical data model, and when I returned to modeling, I anticipated many of the questions I knew the developers needed to know on the physical data model.

This may sound geeky, but I also find myself modeling forms and documents that I encounter in my personal life. For example, I might sketch the data model for a menu while waiting to order food in a restaurant. I remember looking at the label of a bottle of prescription medicine and being surprised how concatenated and multi-valued some of the fields that were printed on the label were. I therefore started sketching the ideal data model to store all of this prescription information.

There are some excellent books to read and websites that contain newsletters and other valuable information that I've listed under the Suggested Reading section. Also, if you visit my Web site, www.stevehoberman.com, you can add your email address to the design challenge list. Once a month, I email a data modeling puzzle to everyone on the list, then I consolidate everyone's responses and publish them in a well-known industry publication.

There are conferences, courses, and data organizations that keep us in touch with the industry. I teach a three-day class on data modeling called the Data Modeling Master Class (www.stevehoberman.com/DataModelingMasterClass.pdf). The annual Data Modeling Zone (www.DataModelingZone.com) is a great way to stay in touch with the community. Also DAMA (www.dama.org) has fabulous resources and networking opportunities.

BOOKS

Adelman S., Moss L., Abai M. 2005. *Data Strategy*, Boston, MA: Addison-Wesley Publishing Company.

Blaha M., 2013. *UML Database Modeling Workbook*, New Jersey: Technics Publications, LLC.

DAMA International 2009. *Data Management Body of Knowledge (DAMA-DMBOK)*, New Jersey: Technics Publications, LLC.

Eckerson, W. 2012. *The Analytical Puzzle*, New Jersey: Technics Publications, LLC.

Hay, D. 2011. *Enterprise Model Patterns*, New Jersey: Technics Publications, LLC.

Hoberman, S. 2001. *The Data Modeler's Workbench,* New York: John Wiley & Sons, Inc.

Hoberman, S., Burbank, D., Bradley C. 2009, *Data Modeling for the Business*, New Jersey: Technics Publications, LLC.

Inmon W., 2011. *Building the Unstructured Data Warehouse*, New Jersey: Technics Publications, LLC.

Kent W., 2012. *Data and Reality 3rd Edition*, New Jersey: Technics Publications, LLC.

Kimball R., Ross M., Thornthwaite W., Mundy J., Becker B. 2008. *The Data Warehouse Lifecycle Toolkit: Practical Techniques for Building Data Warehouse and Business Intelligence Systems*. Second Edition, New York: John Wiley & Sons, Inc.

Marco D., Jennings M. 2004. *Universal Metadata Models,* New York: John Wiley & Sons, Inc.

Maydanchik, A. 2007. *Data Quality Assessment,* New Jersey: Technics Publications, LLC.

Silverston, L. 2001. *The Data Model Resource Book, Revised Edition, Volume 1, A Library of Universal Data Models For All Enterprises,* New York: John Wiley & Sons, Inc.

Silverston, L. 2001. *The Data Model Resource Book, Revised Edition, Volume 2, A Library of Universal Data Models For Industry Types,* New York: John Wiley & Sons, Inc.

Silverston, L. Agnew, P. 2009. *The Data Model Resource Book, Volume 3, Universal Patterns for Data Modeling,* New York: John Wiley & Sons, Inc.

Simsion, G. 2007. *Data Modeling Theory and Practice,* New Jersey: Technics Publications, LLC.

Simsion G., Witt G. 2005. *Data Modeling Essentials, Third Edition,* San Francisco: Morgan Kaufmann Publishers.

WEB SITES

www.dama.org – Conferences, chapter information, and articles

www.datamodelingzone.com – Annual conference on data modeling

www.eLearningCurve.com – offers some great online courses

www.metadata-standards.org/11179 – Formulation of data definition

www.stevehoberman.com – Add your email address to the Design Challenge list to receive modeling puzzles

www.tdan.com – In-depth quarterly newsletter

www.technicspub.com – Publisher of data management books

"Answers" is a strong word. It implies I know *the* answer as opposed to knowing *an* answer, which is closer to the truth. In other words, you may have different and possibly better answers than I, and that would be a very a good thing!

EXERCISE 1: EDUCATING YOUR NEIGHBOR

I find the analogy that I use most frequently is comparing the data model to a blueprint. Most non-technical friends, family, and neighbors understand this analogy. "Just like you need a blueprint to ensure a sound building structure, you need a data model to ensure a sound application." Sometimes I also explain to people that a data model is nothing more than a fancy spreadsheet, which contains not just the spreadsheet columns, but also the business rules binding these columns. If both the blueprint and spreadsheet analogies fail, I quickly change the subject to the other person and ask what they do (and hope they never ask me again!).

EXERCISE 3: CHOOSING THE RIGHT SETTING

In the following table, I checked off the most appropriate settings for each of these scenarios.

1. Explain how a contact management legacy application works to a team of developers

Scope	Abstraction	Time	Function
☒ Dept	☒ Bus clouds	☒ Today	☐ Bus
☐ Org	☐ DB clouds	☐ Tomorrow	☒ App
☐ Industry	☐ On the ground		

2. Explain the key manufacturing concepts to a new hire

Scope	Abstraction	Time	Function
☐ Dept	☐ Bus clouds	☒ Today	☒ Bus
☒ Org	☐ DB clouds	☐ Tomorrow	☐ App
☐ Industry	☒ On the ground		

3. Capture the detailed requirements for a new sales data mart

Scope	Abstraction	Time	Function
☒ Dept	☐ Bus clouds	☐ Today	☒ Bus
☐ Org	☐ DB clouds	☒ Tomorrow	☐ App
☐ Industry	☒ On the ground		

EXERCISE 5: ASSIGNING DOMAINS

Here are the domains for each of the following three attributes.

EMAIL ADDRESS

Based upon information from Wikipedia:

An e-mail address is a string of a subset of characters separated into 2 parts by an "@", a "local-part" and a domain, that is, local-part@domain. The local-part of an e-mail address may be up to 64 characters long and the domain name may have a maximum of 255 characters. However, the maximum length of the entire e-mail address is 254 characters.

The local-part of the e-mail address may use any of these characters:

- *Uppercase and lowercase English letters (a-z, A-Z)*
- *Digits 0 through 9*
- *Characters ! # $ % & ' * + - / = ? ^ _ ` { | } ~*

- *Character . (dot, period, full stop) provided that it is not the first or last character, and provided also that it does not appear two or more times consecutively.*
- *Additionally, quoted-strings (i.e.: "John Doe"@example.com) are permitted, thus allowing characters that would otherwise be prohibited, however they do not appear in common practice.*

GROSS SALES AMOUNT

A format domain of Decimal(15,4). Both negative and positive numbers are acceptable.

COUNTRY CODE

As part of the ISO 3166-1993 standard, **Country Code** is two characters in length, and is a list domain consisting of over 200 values. Here is a partial list:

Code	Definition and Explanation
AD	Andorra
AE	United Arab Emirates
AF	Afghanistan
AG	Antigua & Barbuda
AI	Anguilla
AL	Albania
AM	Armenia
AN	Netherlands Antilles
AO	Angola
AQ	Antarctica
AR	Argentina
AS	American Samoa
AT	Austria
AU	Australia
AW	Aruba
AZ	Azerbaijan
ZM	Zambia
ZR	Zaire
ZW	Zimbabwe
ZZ	Unknown or unspecified country

Just the codes beginning with 'A' or 'Z' are shown. 'ZZ' is an interesting country, and illustrates how easy it is to circumvent a business rule. That is, if we don't know the country and **Country Code** is required, we can always assign a 'ZZ' for 'Unknown'.

EXERCISE 6: READING A MODEL

Recall the model:

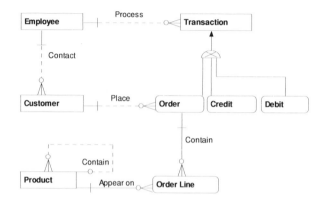

- Each **Employee** may process one or many **Transactions**.
- Each **Transaction** must be processed by one **Employee**.
- Each **Employee** may contact one or many **Customers**.
- Each **Customer** must be contacted by one **Employee**.
- Each **Transaction** may be either an **Order**, **Credit**, or **Debit**.
- Each **Order** is a **Transaction**.
- Each **Credit** is a **Transaction**.
- Each **Debit** is a **Transaction**.
- Each **Customer** may place one or many **Orders**.
- Each **Order** must be placed by one **Customer**.
- Each **Order** may contain one or many **Order Lines**.
- Each **Order Line** must belong to one **Order**.
- Each **Product** may appear on one or many **Order Lines**.
- Each **Order Line** must reference one **Product**.
- Each **Product** may contain one or many **Products**.
- Each **Product** may belong to one **Product**.

EXERCISE 7: CLARIFYING CUSTOMER ID

There are three terms within this definition that require an explanation: *'unique'*, *'identifier'*, and *'Customer'*.

DOCUMENT UNIQUENESS PROPERTIES

The term 'unique' is ambiguous and could easily be interpreted differently by readers of this definition. To maintain clarity and correctness, these questions should be answered within the definition:

- Are identifier values ever reused?
- What is the scope of uniqueness?
- How is the identifier validated?

DOCUMENT THE CHARACTERISTICS OF THE IDENTIFIER

We can describe the actual identifier in more detail including addressing these areas:

- **Purpose.** For example, perhaps the identifier is needed because there are multiple source systems for Customer data, each with their own Id. To enable a common set of data to be held about them, this identifier needed to be created to facilitate integration and guarantee uniqueness across all customers.
- **Business or surrogate key.** Document whether the identifier is meaningful to the business (i.e. the business or natural key) or whether it is a meaningless integer counter (i.e. the surrogate key).
- **Assignment.** Document how a new customer identifier is assigned. The party that is responsible for creating new identifiers should also be mentioned.

DEFINE THE CUSTOMER

Because definitions should stand on their own, we also can define customer within this definition. We can reference the concept definition of customer.

EXERCISE 9: MODIFYING A LOGICAL DATA MODEL

There are two ways to model this situation. The key point with this challenge is to use subtyping and keep **Office First Occupied Date** in the subtype as not null.

OPTION 1

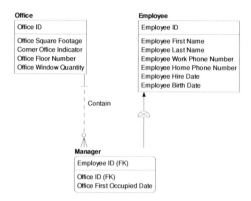

In this model we subtyped **Manager** as a type of **Employee**. All of the attributes and relationships that are specific to a **Manager** are moved to the **Manager** entity. Therefore, the business rule that each **Manager** must reside in one and only one **Office** and each **Office** may contain one or many **Managers** is represented. Also, the **Office First Occupied Date** is now a mandatory field in the **Manager** entity, whereas in the **Employee** entity it would have to be null.

OPTION 2 (A BIT MORE ABSTRACT)

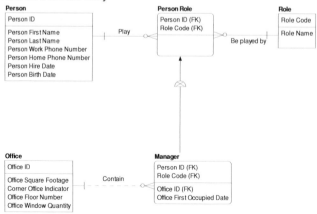

Thinking in more generic terms, we might model that a **Person** can play many **Roles**. One of these **Roles** is a **Manager**. The **Manager** subtype has the additional relationship and mandatory **Office First Occupied Date** that we saw in the previous model. This type of model works out well where application longevity and stability is the goal, such as in a data warehouse or integration hub.

EXERCISE 10: GETTING PHYSICAL WITH SUBTYPES

The following are the three different ways this subtyping structure can be represented on the physical data model.

IDENTITY

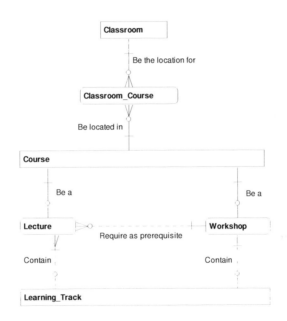

ROLLING UP

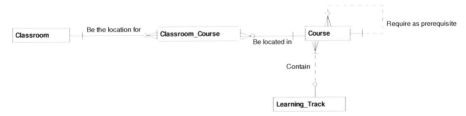

ROLLING DOWN

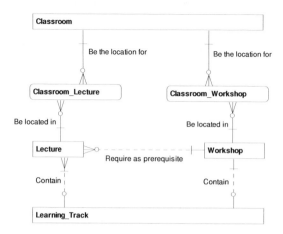

EXERCISE 11: BUILDING THE TEMPLATE

Someone playing the role of functional analyst should be the one responsible for completing the Family Tree. In many organizations, the role 'functional analyst' is performed by a business analyst or a data modeler. This template is often completed in parallel with the logical data modeling effort and often complete at the same time. That is, the logical data analysis phase includes the logical data model and Family Tree.

EXERCISE 12: DETERMINING THE MOST CHALLENGING SCORECARD CATEGORY

I believe Category 2, "How well does the model capture the requirements?" is the most difficult Scorecard category to grade. The business requirements may not be well-defined, or they differ from verbal requirements, or they keep changing usually with the scope expanding instead of contracting.

Abstraction. Brings flexibility to your data models by redefining and combining some of the attributes, entities, and relationships within the model into more generic terms. For example, we may abstract **Employee** and **Consumer** into the more generic concept of **Person**. A **Person** can play many **Roles**, two of which are **Employee** and **Consumer**.

Actor. A role played by a user or application in a specific process, and often depicted as a stick figure on use case diagrams.

Agile. Agile means 'quick' and 'adept'. When applied to application development, agile translates into rapid delivery of high-quality software. Agile usually means there are many project-focused iterations until the project is complete. Proponents of agile say the project-focused approach produces high quality results in much less time than a typical software development methodology. Opponents of agile say the focus of agile is on the project at the expense of the program, meaning usually the enterprise perspective and 'big picture' is not given the attention it requires.

Aggregate. A table that contains the resolution of a one-to-one relationship.

Alternate key. The one or more attributes that uniquely identify a value in an entity and that is not chosen to be *the* unique identifier.

Associative entity. An associative entity is an entity that resolves a many-to-many relationship.

Attribute. Also known as a "data element," an attribute is a property of importance to the business. Its values contribute to identifying, describing, or measuring instances of an entity. The attribute **Claim Number** identifies each claim. The attribute **Student Last Name** describes the last name of each student. The attribute **Gross Sales Amount** measures the monetary value of a transaction.

Bridge table. A table that resolves a many-to-many relationship from the dimension to the meter. In other words, a given meter instance may need to refer to more than one dimension instance. Bridge tables can be shown as the typical resolution of a many-to-many on a logical but may need a different physical structure depending on reporting tools.

Candidate key. The one or many attributes that uniquely identify an entity instance. Candidate keys are either primary or alternate keys.

Cardinality. Defines the number of instances of each entity that can participate in a relationship. It is represented by the symbols that appear on both ends of a relationship line.

Class. A type or category of things with common attributes. Classes are the basis for object-oriented analysis, design and development, where a class is roughly equivalent to an entity with the addition of described functional behavior. The term object is often casually used as a synonym for class.

Class word. The last term in an attribute name such as **Amount**, **Code**, and **Name**. Class words allow for the assignment of common domains.

Concept. A key idea that is both *basic* and *critical* to your audience. "Basic" means this term is probably mentioned many times a day in conversations with the people who are the audience for the model, which includes the people who need to validate the model as well as the people who need to use the model. "Critical" means the business would be very different or non-existent without this concept.

Conceptual Data Model (CDM). A set of symbols and text representing the key concepts and rules binding these key concepts for a specific business or application scope. The CDM represents the business need.

Conformed dimension. Built with the organization in mind, instead of just a particular application, to support drill across queries and enterprise consistency. Conformed dimensions do not need to be identical with each other; they just need to be from the same superset. Conformed dimensions allow the navigator the ability to ask questions that cross multiple marts.

Data model. A set of symbols and text that precisely explains a business information landscape. A box with the word "Customer" within it represents the concept of a real **Customer**, such as `Bob`, `IBM`, or `Walmart`, on a data model. A line represents a relationship between two concepts such as capturing that a **Customer** may own one or many **Accounts**.

Data modeler. A data modeler is one who confirms and documents data requirements. This role performs the data modeling process.

Data modeling. The process of learning about the data; regardless of technology, this process must be performed for a successful application.

Degenerate dimension. A dimension whose attribute(s) have been moved to the fact table. A degenerate dimension is most common when the original dimension contained only a single attribute such as a transaction identifier.

Denormalization. The process of selectively violating normalization rules and reintroducing redundancy into the model. This extra redundancy can reduce data retrieval time and produce a more user-friendly model.

Dependent entity. Also known as a weak entity, a dependent entity is an object of interest to the business that depends on one or many other entities for its existence. The entities that a dependent entity depends on can be independent entities or other dependent entities. A dependent entity is depicted as a rectangle with rounded edges.

Dimension. A subject area whose purpose is to add meaning to the measures. All of the different ways of filtering, sorting, and summing measures make use of dimensions. Dimensions are often, but not exclusively, hierarchies.

Domain. The complete set of all possible values that an attribute can be assigned.

Entity. A collection of information about something that the business deems important and worthy of capture. A noun or noun phrase identifies a specific entity. It fits into one of several categories: who, what, when, where, why, or how.

Entity instance. The occurrences or values of a particular entity. The entity **Customer** may have multiple customer instances with names Bob, Joe, Jane, and so forth. The entity **Account** can have instances of Bob's checking account, Bob's savings account, Joe's brokerage account, and so on.

Extensible Markup Language (XML). A type of data model which displays information in a hierarchy format using human-readable tags, allowing both people and software applications to more easily exchange and share information. XML is both useful and powerful for the same reasons any data model is useful and powerful: it is easy to understand, can be technology-independent, and enables representing complex problems with simple syntax. Similar to distinguishing conceptual data models from logical data models from physical data models, XML distinguishes the data content from formatting (e.g. blue, Arial, 15 point font) from rules.

Fact. *See measure.*

Factless fact. A fact table that does not contain any facts. Factless facts count events by summing relationship occurrences between the dimensions.

Field. The concept of a physical attribute (also called a column).

Foreign key. An attribute that provides a link to another entity. A foreign key allows a database management system to navigate from one entity to another.

Forward engineer. The process of building a new application by starting from the conceptual data model and ending with a database.

Grain. The lowest level of detail available in the meter on a dimensional data model.

Grain Matrix. A spreadsheet, which captures the levels of reporting for each fact or measurement. It is the spreadsheet view of an initial design, which could result in a star schema.

Hierarchy. An arrangement of items (objects, names, values, categories, etc.) in which the items are represented as being "above," "below," or "at the same level as" one another.

Independent entity. Also known as a kernel entity, an independent entity is an object of interest to the business that does not depend on any other entity for its identification. Each occurrence of an independent entity can be identified without referring to any other entity on the model. An independent entity is depicted as a rectangle.

Index. A pointer to something that needs to be retrieved. The index points directly to the place on the disk where the data is stored, thus reducing retrieval time. Indexes work best on attributes whose values are requested frequently but rarely updated.

Inversion Entry (IE). A non-unique index (also known as a secondary key).

Junk dimension. A dimension containing all the possible combinations of a small and somewhat related set of indicators and codes.

Key-value. A NoSQL database that allows the application to store its data in only two columns ("key" and "value") with more complex information sometimes stored within the "value" columns.

Logical Data Model (LDM). The detailed business solution to a business problem. It is how the modeler captures the business requirements without complicating the model with implementation concerns such as software and hardware.

Measure. An attribute in a dimensional data model's meter that helps answer one or more business questions.

Metadata. Text, voice, or image that describes what the audience wants or needs to see or experience. The audience could be a person, group, or software program.

Meter. An entity containing a related set of measures. It is a bucket of common measures. As a group, common measures address a business process such as Profitability, Employee Satisfaction, or Sales.

Model. A set of symbols and text used to make a complex concept easier to grasp.

Natural key. Also known as a business key, a natural key is what the business sees as the unique identifier for an entity.

Network. A many-to-many relationship between entities (or between entity instances).

Normalization. The process of applying a set of rules with the goal of organizing something. With respect to attributes, normalization ensures that every attribute is single valued and provides a fact completely and only about its primary key.

Object. In an object-oriented design, synonymous with a class; an entity that combines descriptions of the common behavior of like instances along with their common data attributes. Objects may be business objects, interface objects or control objects.

Ontology. A formal way of organizing information. It includes putting 'things' into categories and relating these categories with each other. The most quoted definition of an ontology is Tom Gruber's definition: "Explicit specification of a conceptualization." In other words, an ontology is a model – a model being a simplification of something complex in our environment using a standard set of symbols.

NoSQL. NoSQL is a name for the category of databases built on non-relational technology. NoSQL is not a good name for what it represents as it is less about how to query the database (which is where SQL comes in) and more about how the data is stored (which is where relational structures comes in).

Partition. A structure that divides or separates. Specific to the physical design, partitioning is used to break a table into rows, columns, or both. There are two types of partitioning: vertical and horizontal. Vertical partitioning means separating the columns (the attributes) into separate tables. Horizontal means separating rows (the entity instances) into separate tables.

Physical Data Model (PDM). Represents the detailed technical solution. The PDM is the logical data model modified for a specific set of software or hardware. The PDM often gives up perfection for practicality, factoring in real concerns such as speed, space, and security.

Primary key. The one or more attributes that uniquely identify a value in an entity and that is chosen to be *the* unique identifier.

Program. A large, centrally organized initiative that contains multiple projects. It has a start date and, if successful, no end date. Programs can be very complex and require long-term modeling assignments. Examples include a data warehouse or a customer relationship management system.

Project. A complete software development effort, often defined by a set of deliverables with due dates. Examples include a sales data mart, broker trading application, reservations system, or an enhancement to an existing application.

Recursive relationship. A relationship between instances of the same entity. For instance, one organization can report to another organization.

Relational Database Management System. Represents the traditional relational database invented by E. F. Codd at IBM in 1970 and first commercially available in 1979 (which was Oracle) [Wikipedia].

Relational model. Captures how the business works and contains business rules such as "A **Customer** must have at least one **Account**" or "A **Product** must have a **Product Short Name**."

Relationship. Rules are captured on our data model through relationships. A relationship is displayed as a line connecting two entities.

Reverse engineer. The process of understanding an existing application by starting with its database and working up through the modeling levels until a conceptual data model is built.

Secondary key. One or more attributes (if more than one attribute, it is called a composite secondary key) that are accessed frequently and need to be retrieved quickly. A secondary key does not have to be unique, or stable, or always contain a value.

Semi-structured data. Semi-structured data is equivalent to structured data with one minor exception: Semi-structured data requires looking at the data itself to determine structure as opposed to structured data which only requires examining the attribute name. Semi-structured data is one processing step away from structured data.

Snapshot measure. Monitor the impact of events created from a business process such as **Account Balance Amount, Ozone Layer Thickness**, and **Average Survey Question Score**.

Slowly Changing Dimension (SCD). A term for any reference entity where we need to consider how to handle data changes. There are four basic ways to manage history. An SCD of Type 0 means we are only interested in the original state, an SCD of Type 1 means only the most current state, an SCD of Type 2 means the most current along with all history, and an SCD of Type 3 means the most current and some history will be stored.

Snowflake. A physical dimensional modeling structure where each set of tables is implemented separately; very similar in structure to the logical dimensional model.

Spreadsheet. A representation of a paper worksheet containing a grid defined by rows and columns where each cell in the grid can contain text or numbers. The columns often contain different types of information.

Stakeholder. A person who has an interest in the successful completion of a project.

Star schema. The most common physical dimensional data model structure. A star schema results when each set of structures that make up a dimension is flattened into a single structure. The fact table is in the center of the model, and each of the dimensions relate to the fact table at the lowest level of detail.

Structured data. Structured data is any data named with a simple class word. 'Simple' means if data can be broken down, it can only be broken down further through normalization.

Examples:
- Order Entry Date
- Customer Name
- Gross Sales Amount

Subtyping. Grouping together the common properties of entities while retaining what is unique within each entity.

Summarization. A table that contains information at a higher level of granularity than exists in the business.

Surrogate key. A primary key that substitutes for a natural key, which is what the business sees as the unique identifier for an entity. It has no embedded intelligence and is used by IT (and not the business) for integration or performance reasons.

Taxonomy. An ontology in the form of a tree. A tree is when a child only has a single parent and a parent can contain one or more children. If a child can have more than one parent, than the child is typically repeated for each parent. Examples of kinds of taxonomies are product categorizations, supertype/subtype relationships on a relational data model, and dimensional hierarchies on a dimensional data model.

UML (Unified Modeling Language). The dominant modeling language for object-oriented analysis and design, Developed by Jacobsen, Booch and Rumbaugh by consolidating several earlier object-oriented modeling standards.

Unstructured data. Unstructured data is any data named with the complex Text or Object class words. 'Complex' means the data can be broken down into completely different types of data, such as those of simple class words or other complex class words.

Use case. In object-oriented analysis, a work flow scenario defined in order to identify objects, their data and their methods (process steps).

View. A virtual table. It is a dynamic "view" or window into one or more tables (or other views) where the actual data is stored.

Wayfinding. Wayfinding encompasses all of the techniques and tools used by people and animals to find their way from one site to another. If travelers navigate by the stars, for example, the stars are their wayfinding tools. Maps and compasses are also wayfinding tools. All models are wayfinding tools. A map helps a visitor navigate a city. An organization chart helps an employee understand reporting relationships. A blueprint helps an architect communicate building plans.

Bold page numbers indicate where term is defined

15122569R00136

Printed in Great Britain
by Amazon.co.uk, Ltd.,
Marston Gate.